52 WEEKS IN THE STORY THAT CHANGED THE WORLD

EPIC DEVOTIONS

ONE BIG STORY

B&H kids

Nashville TN

For more resources
to help people of all ages
explore the Bible's big story,
visit gospelproject.com

AN EPIC STORY

A story can begin in so many ways. Some are simple, like the familiar "Once upon a time." Others are intriguing, like "It was the best of times, it was the worst of times."[1] And others can even be a little sarcastic, like "There was a boy called Eustace Clarence Scrubb, and he almost deserved it."[2]

There are many great ways to begin a story, but the Bible begins in a way that is better than any other. In fact, it begins in the most perfect way imaginable: "In the beginning" (Genesis 1:1). The Bible is filled with wisdom, songs, and guidance about how to live holy lives. That's not entirely what the Bible is about, though. The Bible is the story of God rescuing human beings. It's a love story, filled with good news for those who hear it. It is a story with one person at its center: Jesus Christ, the Son of God, who came into the world to save people from their sins.

A story like this can only begin with "In the beginning," because that's where it has to begin for us to meet the Hero of the story. He is there in the beginning. In fact, He is there before the beginning. He is on every page as we see the story play out in all of Scripture.

This story is the one story that helps us love God and love others. It is the one story that God's people have been sharing for two thousand years, and God invites us to share and keep sharing until everyone has heard it. The story of the Bible is the story of the gospel—the story that changes everything.

---

1. Charles Dickens, *A Tale of Two Cities* (London: Nisbet, 1902), 3.
2. C. S. Lewis, *The Voyage of the Dawn Treader* (London: Geoffrey Bles, 1952).

HOW TO USE THIS DEVOTIONAL

Each of the devotions in this book has elements to help you get the most out of your reading:

"In the beginning God created the heavens and the earth."
—Genesis 1:1

Key Scripture verse

Scripture reading to go deeper in the Word

READ THE WORD: GENESIS 1:1-2:3

RESCUE FROM SIN

When Cain was born, Adam and Eve were excited, and not just because a new life had come into the world.

Summary of the events that took place in the Bible story

RULE OVER YOUR SIN

Action items to help you dig even deeper

God describes sin as waiting to devour us, but we, like Cain, are called to rule over it. On our own we can't defeat sin, but God doesn't leave us alone; He sent Jesus to rescue us.

Thoughts and questions for discussion

Who is someone you've been angry with or jealous of? Go to that person and ask forgiveness.

And a final memory verse

MEMORIZE ROMANS 5:6

"For while we were still helpless, at the right time, Christ died for the ungodly."

DEVOTIONS

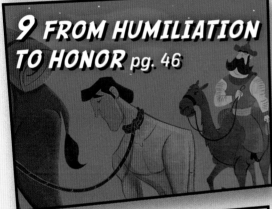
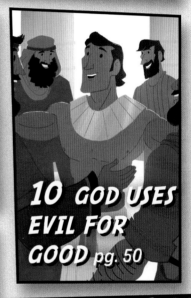

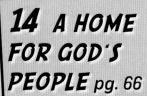

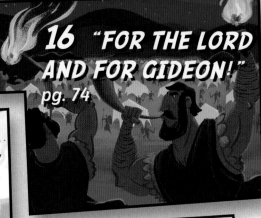

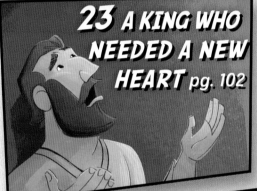

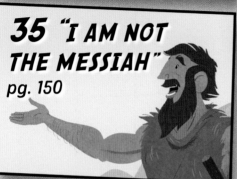

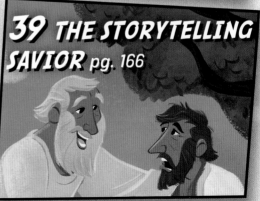

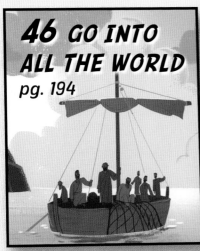

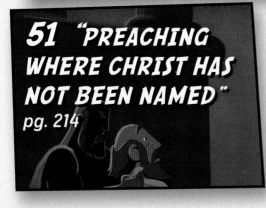
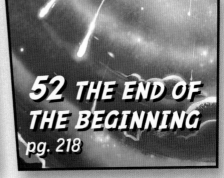

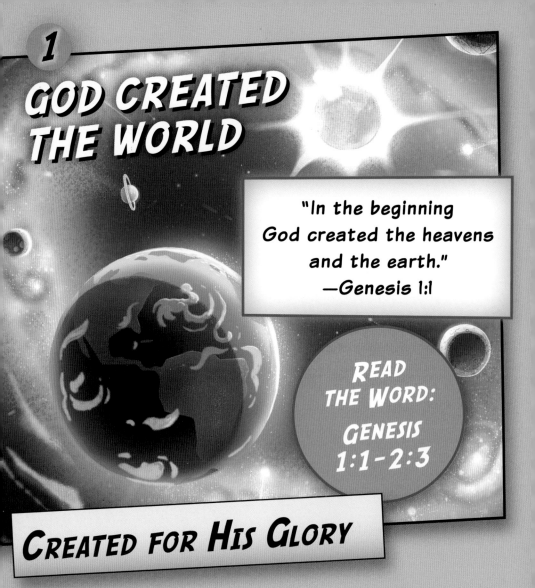

1

GOD CREATED THE WORLD

"In the beginning God created the heavens and the earth."
—Genesis 1:1

READ THE WORD: GENESIS 1:1-2:3

CREATED FOR HIS GLORY

Most of the time, when we're familiar with a story, we assume we know what it says. The creation story is one like that. You may have heard it many times before. There's a lot going on in it—especially when you start thinking about what was there *before* the beginning.

Before the beginning, there was nothing—nothing but God. Before anything was made, God already was. And He made everything. With a word, God made the day and night; the land and sea; the sun and moon; plants and animals . . . and even the stars. Finally, God made people:

human beings, who were made to bear His image. He formed the first man out of dirt with His own hands. He breathed life into him. Then He made a companion for the man from the man's rib, a woman. The first people were His representatives in the world He had made. They, like everything else in the world, were made to glorify Him—to show the world that God is amazing. After God finished creating everything, He looked at all He had made, and called it very good. Then He rested, because His work of creation was finished. But the Bible's epic story was only beginning.

CREATED BY AND FOR THE SON

God wasn't alone in the beginning. There was another who was with God and who was God. The Bible calls Him "the Word" (John 1:1), and later reveals another name: Jesus. Jesus is "the image of the invisible God," and "the exact expression of his nature" (Colossians 1:15; Hebrews 1:3). Everything God made was made by Jesus, through Jesus and for Jesus. When we glorify God, we also want to glorify His Son, Jesus, who came into the world to save us from our sins.

GIVE HIM GLORY

When God created everything to give Him glory, that included you (Genesis 1:26–28)! That doesn't mean it's always easy.

Think about a few of your favorite, and even least favorite, things to do. Thank God that we can use what we enjoy for His glory, and ask Him to help us do the things we don't enjoy for His glory too.

One of the ways we give God glory is by telling others the good news of Jesus's death and resurrection. Think of one person you know who needs to hear about Jesus. Then tell that person all about Him!

MEMORIZE
COLOSSIANS 1:16

"For everything was created by him, in heaven and on earth, the visible and the invisible, whether thrones or dominions or rulers or authorities—all things have been created through him and for him."

2

THE DAY EVERYTHING WENT WRONG

> "I will put hostility between you and the woman, and between your offspring and her offspring. He will strike your head, and you will strike his heel."—Genesis 3:15

READ THE WORD: GENESIS 3:1-24

THE FIRST EXPERIENCE OF SHAME

In the beginning, God's creation was perfect . . . but it didn't stay that way. A serpent approached the first woman and tempted her to break the one command God had given Adam and Eve. They were not to eat fruit from the tree of the knowledge of good and evil; if they did, they would "die." But the serpent was very cunning. He told the woman that they would become like God if they ate that fruit—he deceived her. The woman ate and also gave the fruit to her husband.

Then, for the very first time, Adam and Eve felt ashamed. They didn't want God to see them, so they hid from Him among the trees.

But God found them. And because of their disobedience, God said work would be very difficult, childbirth would be painful, and sin would prevent men and women from treating one another with respect and dignity. He cast them out of His garden forever, placing an angel armed with a fiery sword at its gate. Their perfect life was lost.

THE FIRST GLIMPSE OF HOPE

First, humans were cast out of the garden, broken and ashamed, but they were also given hope. When God explained the consequences of their sin, He also gave them good news: they would have an "offspring" (Genesis 3:15)! This Child would one day destroy the serpent—although it would cost Him greatly. The Bible reveals that Jesus is this promised Son (Luke 3:23–38). He destroyed the serpent's works through His death and resurrection, and He will destroy the serpent once and for all when He returns to make all things new (Revelation 20:10).

CAST OUT SHAME

We all experience the effects of sin today, both because of our nature and by our own choices. While we might feel shame over our sin, God wants us to live in hope because of Jesus.

God said that hostility would exist between people because of sin. How have you seen your relationships hurt because of your sin and others'?

The gospel replaces shame with hope. Who needs you to hear the gospel's message of hope from you?

MEMORIZE ROMANS 5:19

"For just as through one man's disobedience the many were made sinners, so also through the one man's obedience the many will be made righteous."

3
SIN CROUCHES AT THE DOOR

"If you do what is right, won't you be accepted? But if you do not do what is right, sin is crouching at the door. Its desire is for you, but you must rule over it."
—Genesis 4:7

DEVOURED BY SIN

READ THE WORD: GENESIS 4:1-26

Away from the garden, Adam and Eve, the first humans, started a family. They had a son, Cain, and then another, Abel; they would later come to have more children. When Cain and Abel grew up, they offered sacrifices to the Lord. Cain, a farmer, brought some of the produce of the land. Abel, a shepherd, brought the first born of his flock. God was pleased with Abel's offering, but paid no attention to Cain's.

Cain was furious, but God spoke to him and commanded him to set aside his anger. Sin was crouching at the door, waiting to devour Cain.

Cain didn't listen to God. Instead, he called Abel out to a field and killed him. When his sin was discovered, Cain was sent away, cursed to be a restless wanderer for the rest of his life.

RESCUE FROM SIN

When Cain was born, Adam and Eve were excited, and not just because a new life had come into the world. They remembered God's promise that one of their offspring would destroy the serpent. Cain, however, was not the promised Rescuer. Instead, the world's first child was also its first murderer. The Rescuer would not come until centuries later, when, at the right time, Jesus Christ came into the world to save sinners (Romans 5:6).

RULE OVER YOUR SIN

God describes sin as crouching at the door, waiting to devour us, but we, like Cain, are called to rule over it. On our own we can't defeat sin, but God doesn't leave us alone; He sent Jesus to rescue us.

It is impossible for us to resist temptation and sin without God's help. Pray that God would help you live faithfully.

Who is someone you've been angry with or jealous of? Go to that person and ask forgiveness.

MEMORIZE ROMANS 5:6

"While we were still helpless, at the right time, Christ died for the ungodly."

4

A WARNING, A FLOOD, AND A PROMISE

> "The LORD regretted that he had made man on the earth, and he was deeply grieved."—Genesis 6:6

READ THE WORD: GENESIS 6-9

GOD'S JUDGMENT ON THE WORLD

As years turned into decades and then centuries, Adam and Eve's family—the human race—grew. So did their sin. God was grieved by their wickedness and regretted making them. He decided to punish their sin by sending a flood, one that would cover the entire earth. No one would be spared except Noah and his family. Noah found favor in the eyes of the Lord; he was a righteous man who walked with God. God commanded him to build an ark, a massive ship that would hold Noah's family and pairs of every kind of animal. Noah did all that God commanded.

When the ark was finished and all the animals were on board, the rain began and didn't stop for forty days. Water covered the surface of the earth for one hundred fifty days before it was safe to leave the ark. When Noah returned to dry land, he built an altar and made an offering to God. The Lord was pleased and promised to never again destroy the earth with a flood. He gave a sign that would forever remind us, every time we see it, of that promise: *a rainbow*.

GOD'S GRACE FOR THE WORLD

The flood didn't end humanity's sin problem. Sin continued in the hearts of Noah and his descendants (all the relatives that came after him). But despite their continued rebellion, God had not failed. He was continuing His plan of sending the One to whom the ark pointed—Jesus, the promised Rescuer. Noah's family found refuge (a safe place) in the ark. Today, everyone who believes in Jesus finds refuge from God's final judgment of sin.

GOD'S FAVOR TO YOU

Noah was a righteous man, but he was not a perfect man. He needed to be saved the same way we all do: by God's grace through faith (Ephesians 2:8).

The story of the flood reminds us that God takes sin seriously. Do you take your sin as seriously as you should? Why or why not?

God is patient. He gives opportunities to turn to Him through faith in His Son for forgiveness of sins. Have you put your faith in Jesus?

MEMORIZE
EPHESIANS 2:8

"For you are saved by grace through faith, and this is not from yourselves; it is God's gift."

5

THE PROMISE AND BLESSING

"And all the peoples on earth will be blessed through you."
—Genesis 12:3

READ THE WORD:
GENESIS 12: 15: 17

THE PROMISE TO ONE MAN

Abram was 75 years old when God made him a promise: God would lead Abram to a land not his own. There God would make him a great nation, and the whole world would be blessed through him. Abram didn't understand how this could be. To be a nation, he would have to have descendants—children. But he and his wife, Sarai, had no children. Even so, Abram believed. He went to the land God showed him, the land of Canaan.

In Canaan, God told Abram that this land would belong to his offspring forever. But still Abram had no children. And still, he believed. Years later, God made a covenant, an unbreakable promise, with Abram: Abram would have a child, and not only one, but he would have as many descendants as stars in the sky. This promise would be fulfilled no matter what. Each time God spoke with Abram, He renewed the promise. He gave a sign that Abram's family was set apart from the rest of humanity: He gave Abram and Sarai new names—Abraham and Sarah. When Sarah was 90 years old and Abraham was 100, God gave them a child—Isaac.

THE BLESSING FOR ALL THE WORLD

Through all the years he waited, Abraham believed God would fulfill His promise. When Isaac was born, Abraham's faith was shown not to be in vain. Isaac was the child God had promised, Abraham's heir, and the one through whom God would bless all the nations. He would do it through another promised Child, a Child who was a descendant of Isaac and Abraham, a Child promised long before, in the garden. A Child who would crush the head of the serpent and rescue God's people from the curse of sin. Jesus Christ, the Son of God, who died to take away the sins of the world, was that promised Child.

WHILE YOU WAIT

Today, God's people wait for God to fulfill His promise: for Jesus to return and for the world to be made new, so we can live forever with God. We don't know when it will happen, but we have faith that it will.

Think about the promises God makes in Scripture. Is it hard to wait for them to come to pass? Why?

God blesses people all over the world. Take a moment and pray for missionaries in other countries who are spreading the good news about Jesus.

MEMORIZE ROMANS 4:3

"For what does the Scripture say? Abraham believed God, and it was credited to him for righteousness."

6
THE SON, THE RAM, AND THE SACRIFICE

"God himself will provide the lamb for the burnt offering, my son."
— Genesis 22:8

THE SON WHO WAS OFFERED

One day, God commanded Abraham to take his son, Isaac, to the top of a mountain and offer him as a sacrifice. Abraham was in shock; he didn't understand how God could ask such a thing. Even so, he obeyed.

When they arrived at the mountain, Isaac carried the firewood on his back. Abraham carried the knife. But Isaac noticed there was no lamb for the sacrifice. As they climbed, Isaac asked about it. "God will provide the lamb," Abraham replied. He believed it would be so, despite not knowing how.

They built the altar and arranged the firewood. Then Abraham placed Isaac on the altar. He raised his knife, ready to obey God. Just then, the angel of the Lord commanded him to stop. Immediately, Abraham dropped the knife and freed his son. The father and son heard something rustling in the bushes. It was a ram. God had provided a sacrifice—a substitute for Abraham's one and only son.

THE FATHER'S GREATER SACRIFICE

God's command to sacrifice Isaac was a test of Abraham's faith, to see if he trusted God enough not to hold back what he loved most. Abraham's willingness to sacrifice his one and only son also pointed forward to the day when another Father would sacrifice His one and only Son, Jesus. But unlike Isaac, no substitute was provided for Jesus because He *was* the substitute being offered to pay for the sins of the world. Through Him, all the nations of the world are blessed. Everyone who believes in Jesus finds forgiveness of their sins and are adopted into God's family as His beloved sons and daughters.

OFFERING WHAT MATTERS MOST

God's test of Abraham is hard for us to understand, but it helps us understand the sacrifice God would later make and gives us a picture of faithful sacrifice. God calls His people to hold nothing back from Him—even the things we love most.

Pray and ask God to help you be willing to give up anything He asks you to.

God uses everyone who believes in Jesus to show His love and bless the world. What is one thing you can do this week to show God's love to people in your community?

MEMORIZE GALATIANS 3:16

"Now the promises were spoken to Abraham and to his seed. He does not say 'and to seeds,' as though referring to many, but referring to one, and to your seed, who is Christ."

7

STOLEN BLESSINGS

"May peoples serve you and nations bow in worship to you. Be master over your relatives; may your mother's sons bow in worship to you. Those who curse you will be cursed, and those who bless you will be blessed."
—Genesis 27:29

READ THE WORD: GENESIS 24-25, 27-28

THE BLESSING STOLEN

When Abraham died, God appeared to Isaac and made a covenant with him—the same covenant God had made with Isaac's father. Isaac had two sons, Esau and Jacob. Esau was the oldest. He loved to hunt and fish and was his father's favorite. Jacob was quiet and clever and preferred to stay in the tents with his mother.

One day, Esau returned from hunting and saw Jacob
cooking a lentil stew. Tired and hungry, Esau asked for
a bowl. Jacob agreed, but on one condition: Esau must
give him his birthright—his inheritance and status in the
family. Esau agreed. Then he ate, and his hunger was
satisfied, but he became bitter toward his brother for
taking his birthright. But Jacob knew that Esau still held
something even *more* valuable: their father's blessing.

One day, when Isaac was old and could no longer see,
Jacob pretended to be Esau in order to receive the blessing that was supposed to go to the oldest son. His father
blessed him, and Jacob left. When Esau returned from
hunting, he and Isaac learned of Jacob's deceit. They were
furious, and Esau was determined to kill his brother. But
Jacob escaped to the land of Ur, the land of his ancestors.

THE COVENANT CONTINUED

On the way to Ur, Jacob stopped to rest at Bethel. There, God made a covenant with him—the same covenant God had made with Abraham and Isaac. Jacob would have many descendants, and God would bless them. Jacob's family grew and became a great nation, and from his descendants came the One whom God had promised from the beginning: Jesus, the promised Rescuer, who would take away the sins of the world.

IMPERFECT PEOPLE IN GOD'S PERFECT PLAN

Jacob was hardly worthy of the blessing He received, but God uses the imperfect to carry out His plans.

Have you ever tried to take something that didn't belong to you? What happened? How did it make you feel?

MEMORIZE ROMANS 2:11

"For there is no favoritism with God."

God blesses us so we can bless others—to show God's love, kindness, and grace to them. How can you bless someone this week?

8

GOD'S KINDNESS TO A SCHEMER

WRESTLING WITH GOD

It had been twenty years since Jacob left Canaan in fear for his life. In that time, God blessed him with a family and many possessions. Jacob's uncle, though, was as crafty as his nephew. He took every opportunity to cheat Jacob, including changing his wages ten times. Finally, Jacob left, along with his family and possessions. He decided to return to Canaan, even though it meant facing Esau, his brother, once again. He sent messengers ahead to Esau and sent his family away, out of harm's way.

"Your name will no longer be Jacob ... It will be Israel because you have struggled with God and with men and have prevailed."
—Genesis 32:28

READ THE WORD: GENESIS 29-33

When Jacob was alone, a Man appeared out of nowhere and wrestled with him. They fought until the early morning hours when, finally, the Man struck Jacob's hip and dislocated it. Despite the pain, Jacob refused to loosen his grip. He would not yield unless the Man blessed him. The Man did, first asking Jacob's name, then giving him a new one: Israel, because he had struggled with God and with men and overcome. Then the Man disappeared, leaving Israel alone to walk with a limp for the rest of his days, a reminder of God's mercy to him.

GOD'S MERCY TO JACOB

The blessing Jacob received was not one he deserved. He could not scheme his way into receiving it, the way he had stolen the blessing from his father. This blessing could only be freely given. It was a blessing God had always intended for him, one that led to the blessing of all the people of the earth. Israel's descendants grew into a great nation, and from that nation came the blessing all Scripture points to—Jesus, the Man who is God, who would give His life to bless all who would believe.

GOD'S MERCY TO YOU

Blessing from God cannot be earned, any more than it can be stolen from another. We cannot earn God's kindness. Instead, God freely and joyfully blesses us with it in Christ.

Has someone ever tried to cheat you out of something that belonged to you? What happened?

What is one way you can bless someone you know today?

MEMORIZE ROMANS 4:5

"But to the one who does not work, but believes on him who declares the ungodly to be righteous, his faith is credited for righteousness."

9

FROM HUMILIATION TO HONOR

READ
THE WORD:
GENESIS
37, 39-41

"Listen to this dream I had ..."
–Genesis 37:6

DEALING WITH A DREAMER

Joseph was one of Jacob's sons. One day, Joseph told his brothers about a strange dream. In it, his brothers and father bowed down to him, as if he were a king. This made Joseph's brothers mad. He was already their father's favorite. Now, he was having visions of ruling over them all? They decided they would do something about the dreamer. They tore off his robe, threw him in a well, and sold him to slave traders.

Joseph was taken to Egypt and ended up in jail although he had done nothing wrong.

Pharaoh was the ruler of Egypt. In prison, Joseph met Pharaoh's cupbearer and baker, who had strange dreams they didn't understand. They shared their dreams with Joseph, and God helped Joseph interpret them. Joseph asked the cupbearer to speak to Pharaoh for him, but the cupbearer forgot all about Joseph—until Pharaoh started dreaming too. When the cupbearer told Pharaoh about Joseph, he was brought to Pharaoh's court and asked to explain the dreams. In them, seven healthy cows were eaten by seven sickly ones, and seven plump heads of grain were swallowed by seven withered ones. Joseph said the two dreams were one: Egypt would experience seven years of great harvest, followed by seven years of famine. Joseph advised Pharaoh to store up a fifth of the grain from the good years to eat during the famine. Pharaoh agreed and appointed Joseph as overseer of the project and all Egypt.

REJECTION AND HONOR

Joseph's dream did not turn out quite as he expected—at least, not yet. Instead of being honored, he was humiliated. He was rejected by his brothers, sold into slavery for twenty pieces of silver, falsely accused of crimes, and imprisoned. But through it all, the Lord was with Joseph, and He blessed all that he did and exalted him. In a similar way, Jesus did not receive honor as God but, instead, humbled Himself and became a human being. He was rejected by His brothers. He was accused of crimes He did not commit. He was sold for thirty pieces of silver. He was beaten and ultimately killed. But through it all, God was with Jesus, and the Lord blessed all He did. Now Jesus rules over an eternal kingdom, one that will never end.

GOD'S FAVOR IN DIFFICULT TIMES

We don't always understand why we experience the troubles we do in our lives, but we can be sure that God will work them out for our good.

How helpful is it for you to know that God is with you even in difficult times? Why?

Who do you know who is going through a difficult situation? How can you encourage that person to not lose hope?

MEMORIZE
PHILIPPIANS 2:7

"He emptied himself by assuming the form of a servant, taking on the likeness of humanity."

10

GOD USES EVIL FOR GOOD

"You planned evil against me; God planned it for good to bring about the present result—the survival of many people."—Genesis 50:20

READ THE WORD: GENESIS 42-50

A FAMILY RESTORED

During the great famine, Jacob, Joseph's father, learned that there was grain in Egypt and sent his sons to purchase some. When they arrived, they bowed before the Pharaoh's overseer—their own brother—but didn't recognize him. Joseph, however, recognized them and decided to test them. He accused them of being spies and told them to go home and get their youngest brother—and they were not to return without him. When their grain ran out, their father asked them to go back to Egypt for more.

The brothers reminded him that they *couldn't* return without Benjamin, their youngest brother. Reluctantly, Jacob agreed, and they went to Egypt again. When they arrived, Joseph commanded they be brought to his home for a feast. There, he put them to one final test. He hid a silver cup in Benjamin's bags. After they left, Joseph told his servant to catch them and accuse them of stealing it. The brothers were brought back, and Joseph said that Benjamin must now be his slave. Their brother Judah begged to be taken in Benjamin's place. Hearing his brother's plea, Joseph revealed his identity. His brothers were terrified, but Joseph told them not to be afraid because what they'd meant for evil, God used for good. When Pharaoh learned of Joseph's family, he encouraged them all to come to Egypt to be with Joseph. Jacob and all his descendants moved to Egypt, where they remained for four hundred years.

A GREAT PROMISE

Before he died, Jacob blessed his sons and told his son
Judah that kings would come from his family. Centuries
later, Israel's most faithful human king, David, would be
a descendant of Judah, and from his family would come
another King, One who rules forever—Jesus, the One who
takes away the sins of the world.

USING OUR CIRCUMSTANCES FOR GOOD

God is not just with us when we experience difficult situations. He uses them to accomplish His purposes.

How challenging is it to believe that God uses our circumstances for good? Why?

Do you know someone who is facing difficult circumstances? Encourage them with the truth you've learned this week: God uses evil for good.

MEMORIZE PSALM 138:8

"The LORD will fulfill his purpose for me. LORD, your faithful love endures forever; do not abandon the work of your hands."

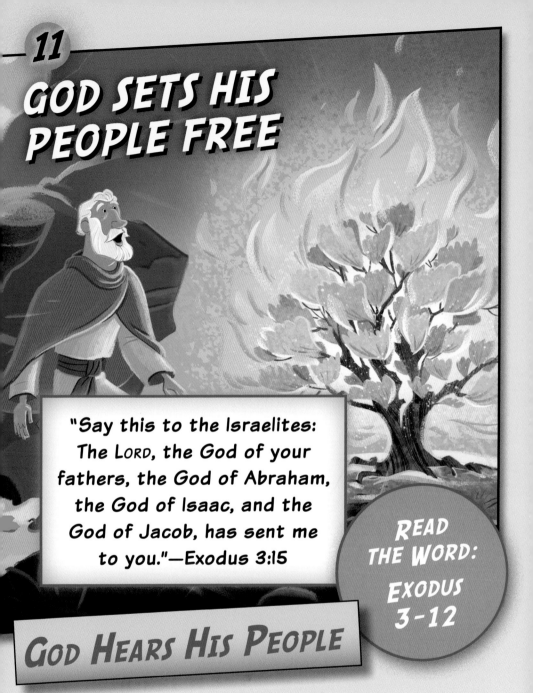

11

GOD SETS HIS PEOPLE FREE

"Say this to the Israelites: The LORD, the God of your fathers, the God of Abraham, the God of Isaac, and the God of Jacob, has sent me to you."—Exodus 3:15

READ THE WORD: EXODUS 3-12

GOD HEARS HIS PEOPLE

Moses couldn't believe what was happening: a voice, the voice of God, was speaking to him from a burning bush, one that wasn't being consumed. After Joseph died, the Egyptians made the Israelites their slaves. The Israelites cried out for God to help, and God heard them.

God commanded Moses to go to Egypt and tell Pharaoh to release the Israelites from slavery so they could worship Him. Moses obeyed and went. Each time Moses spoke, Pharaoh refused to release the Israelites. God sent nine plagues as a warning to Egypt, but no plague softened Pharaoh's heart. He refused to let Israel go.

Then God was ready for one final plague: the firstborn son of every house in Egypt would die. No household would be spared except those who painted their doorways with the blood of a lamb. The Israelites made their sacrifices, painted their doorways, and waited. Night came. Suddenly, cries were heard from every home in Egypt as death came to each one—including Pharaoh's palace! But the Israelites were safe. This time, when Moses went to the palace, Pharaoh released Israel. The Israelites walked out of Egypt and into the wilderness, led by a pillar of fire by night and a pillar of cloud by day.

GOD SAVES HIS PEOPLE

God spared the Israelites from judgment by requiring the blood of a lamb as a sacrifice in their place. The Passover lamb pointed forward to Jesus's sacrifice on the cross in the place of sinful people. Jesus is the Lamb of God, and when we have faith in Him, we are spared from God's final judgment of sin through His death and resurrection.

TRUSTING IN THE POWER OF GOD

The plagues are meant to remind us that God is more powerful than anyone or anything. Only He has the power to save people from sin.

Do you believe God is powerful enough to work in your life? Why?

God wants us to tell others about Jesus, the One who gave His life for us. Who can you tell about Jesus this week?

MEMORIZE
1 PETER 1:18–19

"For you know that you were redeemed . . . not with perishable things like silver or gold, but with the precious blood of Christ, like that of an unblemished and spotless lamb."

12

GOD DELIVERS HIS PEOPLE

READ THE WORD: EXODUS 13-14

"That day the LORD saved Israel from the power of the Egyptians."
—Exodus 14:30

DELIVERED THROUGH THE WATER

Soon after the people of Israel left Egypt, Pharaoh became angry. He sent his army after the Israelites to force them to return to Egypt—and slavery. Pharaoh caught up with the Israelites at the Red Sea. The people were worried. Some cried out and demanded to know if God had led them there to die! As the people panicked, God told Moses to lift his hand toward the sea.

When he did, the water parted, revealing dry land for the Israelites to cross over. The Egyptian army arrived just as the last of the Israelites were crossing to the other side of the sea. The soldiers began to cross too. Then God brought the water crashing back down to destroy Pharaoh's army. Egypt was defeated, and Israel began its journey toward the promised land—the land God had promised Abraham and his descendants centuries before.

JUDGMENT POURED OUT ON ANOTHER

God delivered His people through the waters of the Red Sea—waters of judgment for the Egyptian army. God still delivers people today, through Jesus's death and resurrection. Jesus never sinned, but the judgment our sin deserves was poured out on Him on the cross. Through faith in Him, we are delivered from judgment into new life as a member of God's family.

FAITH IN GOD'S GOODNESS

Maintaining hope in difficult situations requires faith in the goodness and character of God. He wants us to know that everything He does is for His glory and our good.

Do you have trouble staying hopeful in difficult situations? Why?

Because of the gospel, Christians have every reason to have hope. How can you share this hope with one person this week?

MEMORIZE
HEBREWS 11:29

"By faith they crossed the Red Sea as though they were on dry land. When the Egyptians attempted to do this, they were drowned."

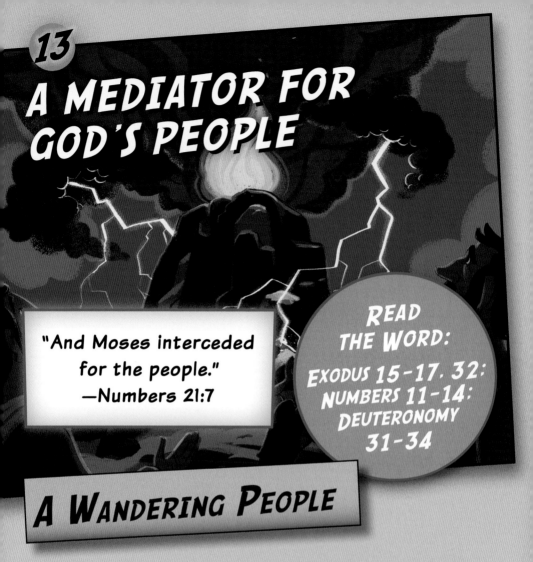

13

A MEDIATOR FOR GOD'S PEOPLE

"And Moses interceded for the people."
—Numbers 21:7

READ THE WORD: EXODUS 15-17. 32: NUMBERS 11-14: DEUTERONOMY 31-34

A WANDERING PEOPLE

Israel wandered in the wilderness for forty years, and for forty years, they grumbled, complained, and were unfaithful to the God who had delivered them from slavery. When they needed food and God provided it by making bread fall from the sky every day, they demanded meat. When Moses was slow to return from speaking with God, the people made a golden calf and worshiped it. When God brought them to the edge of the promised land a few months after leaving Egypt, they refused to enter because they feared the people who lived there. They could not see that God's provision was enough for them.

Despite their sin, God showed the people mercy. When they grumbled about having no water, Moses struck a rock and water poured out. When they worshiped idols, Moses pleaded for their lives before God. When one generation refused to enter the promised land, God promised that the next generation would. Moses always mediated—or spoke to God—on the people's behalf. Even when he was prevented from entering the promised land, Moses continued to represent the people. Before he died, Moses told them that, one day, God would send another mediator like him and commanded that they *listen* to this Mediator.

A BETTER MEDIATOR than MOSES

Moses was Israel's mediator, representing Israel before God and communicating on behalf of God to Israel. He was faithful and humble, but he couldn't solve their sin problem because he was a sinner too. God would send another Mediator, one who was greater than Moses. Jesus, who is both God and human, is the one Mediator between God and humanity. Through faith in Him, we have peace with God and are welcomed into His family forever.

INTERCEDING FOR OTHERS

Right now, Jesus is standing before God the Father, interceding on behalf of all who trust Him. We can bring our needs to Him, knowing that He will respond.

What part of your life are you most tempted to grumble and complain about? Pray and ask God to help you to resist the temptation to complain and to give you a grateful heart.

Jesus wants us to pray for others just as He prays for us. Who can you pray for today?

MEMORIZE 1 TIMOTHY 2:5

"For there is one God and one mediator between God and humanity, the man Christ Jesus."

14

A HOME FOR GOD'S PEOPLE

"Fear the LORD and worship him in sincerity and truth."
—Joshua 24:14

READ THE WORD: JOSHUA 1–11, 24

GOD GAVE THEM VICTORY

Moses was dead, and Joshua was preparing to lead the Israelites into the promised land. It would not be easy, but God was with Joshua. "Be strong and courageous," God told him. "I will be with you wherever you go." Then God proved it.

Joshua sent spies to the city of Jericho to learn what they were up against. They discovered that its inhabitants were panicking because they knew God had given the land to Israel.

So Israel attacked the city—but not in a way anyone would expect. Once a day for six days, they marched silently around the city while their priests blew trumpets. On the seventh day, they marched seven times, and when the priests blew their horns for the last time, the people shouted. The walls of Jericho collapsed, and the Israelites took the city. As they continued their conquest, every enemy fell until only a handful remained.

Years passed, and Joshua's time as leader came to an end. Just before he died, he gathered all the people together and reminded them of all God had done for them. Then he gave them one final command: fear God and worship Him only.

THE GREATER JOSHUA TO COME

Joshua was faithful as he led the people to victory in the promised land, the land God gave them. Centuries later, another person would come to lead God's people into victory over a greater enemy—sin and death. Jesus, the promised Rescuer, would not only remind God's people that God saves, He would also be their salvation by giving His life in their place.

FEAR GOD AND WORSHIP HIM ONLY

God's faithfulness to His people in the past is a reminder that He will be faithful to us now and forever. Just as Israel was called to fear and worship God only, we are called to do the same.

As a family, talk about some of the ways God has been faithful to you. Pray and thank Him for His faithfulness.

"Joshua" means "the Lord Saves." Who do you know who needs to know this truth today?

MEMORIZE JOHN 16:33

"I have told you these things so that in me you may have peace. You will have suffering in this world. Be courageous! I have conquered the world."

15

THE VICTORY BELONGS TO ANOTHER

"Another generation rose up who did not know the LORD or the works he had done for Israel."
—Judges 2:10

READ THE WORD: JUDGES 4-5

GOD RESCUES HIS PEOPLE

After Joshua died, the Israelites began to worship false gods, breaking their vow to worship only God. They did not know the Lord or all He had done for Israel. Because of the people's sin, God allowed the rulers of the surrounding nations to attack them. One of those was King Jabin of Canaan who oppressed them twenty years!

Eventually, God's people cried out to Him for help, and God answered through Deborah, a prophetess, who was a judge over the nation.

Barak, the commander of Israel's army, went to see Deborah. She told him to take an army of 10,000 into battle against Sisera, the leader of Canaan's troops. Barak said he would, but only if Deborah came as well. She agreed, but told him that the victory would belong not to him, but to another.

The battle was fierce, and the Lord threw Sisera and his forces into a panic. Sisera ran from the battle and hid in the tents of a woman named Jael. She encouraged Sisera to rest, and while he was sleeping, she crept over to Sisera and killed him with a tent peg and a mallet. The victory belonged to her, and God's word was fulfilled. Barak arrived and found Sisera dead. He and Deborah rejoiced and gave thanks to God, and Israel enjoyed forty years of peace.

THE GREATER SAVIOR TO COME

Deborah and Barak led Israel into a time of peace, but it would not last. The nation would, again, turn away from God and worship the idols of their neighbors. They needed a greater victory, one that would break sin's hold on their hearts forever—a victory that would come centuries later when Jesus gave His life on the cross and rose again.

VICTORY BELONGS TO ANOTHER

We should thank God every time we overcome temptation and resist sin, because Jesus won the battle that makes it possible.

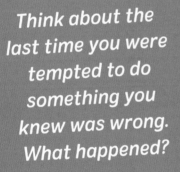

Think about the last time you were tempted to do something you knew was wrong. What happened?

How do you see God making a friend or family member more like Jesus? Tell them what you see and thank God together.

MEMORIZE
PHILIPPIANS 2:12-13

"Work out your own salvation with fear and trembling. For it is God who is working in you both to will and to work according to his good purpose."

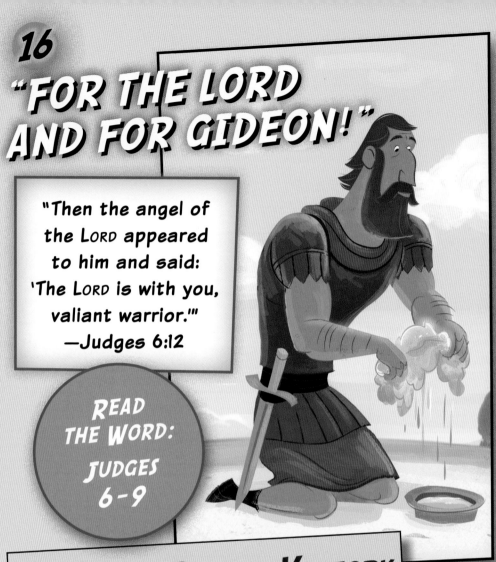

16

"FOR THE LORD AND FOR GIDEON!"

"Then the angel of the LORD appeared to him and said: 'The LORD is with you, valiant warrior.'"
—Judges 6:12

READ THE WORD: JUDGES 6-9

GOD GAVE GIDEON VICTORY

Once again, Israel sinned against God by worshiping false gods. This time, God allowed the Midianites to oppress them. The angel of the Lord appeared to a man named Gideon and told him that God would use Gideon to rescue His people from Midian. Gideon thought it had to be a mistake. So he asked God for a sign. Then he asked for another, and when God did what he asked both times, Gideon went to face the Midianites with 32,000 troops.

But God said this was too many soldiers, so He decreased the army to just three hundred. Victory would be impossible with such a small group, unless God gave them the victory. Outside the Midianite camp, Gideon split his army into three groups and commanded that each man blow a trumpet, smash a pitcher with a torch inside, and shout, "For the Lord and for Gideon!" When they did, the sound was so loud that it threw the Midianites into such confusion that they fought each other. God gave Gideon victory over Midian, and Israel was at peace once again.

An Even More Unbelievable Victory to Come

By any human understanding, Gideon should not have been able to defeat the Midianites. But Gideon was victorious because God gave him the victory. In this, God gave us a picture of a greater victory still to come, a victory even more unbelievable than three hundred men defeating an army. That victory would come when Jesus, the Son of God, gave His life on the cross to defeat sin and death. All who trust in Him are forgiven of their sins and enjoy peace with God forever.

"WHO AM I?"

God uses the unexpected to fulfill His plans. Nothing about our family or our past actions can stop Him from using us to help people see how great He is.

Do you believe that God uses unexpected and ordinary people to fulfill His plans? Why?

MEMORIZE ISAIAH 43:7

"Everyone who bears my name and is created for my glory[,] I have formed them; indeed, I have made them."

Pray and ask God to show you an opportunity to show His greatness this week.

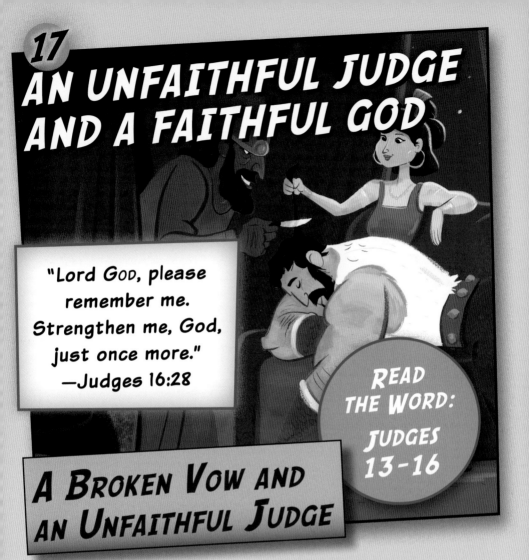

17

AN UNFAITHFUL JUDGE AND A FAITHFUL GOD

"Lord GOD, please remember me. Strengthen me, God, just once more."
—Judges 16:28

READ THE WORD: JUDGES 13–16

A BROKEN VOW AND AN UNFAITHFUL JUDGE

Samson was a Nazarite—a person consecrated to God's service from birth. As part of his vow, he was not to touch anything dead or cut his hair, and God blessed Samson with great strength to defeat Israel's enemies, the Philistines. But Samson was not faithful to his vow. He tore apart a lion with his bare hands. He killed many Philistines using a donkey's jawbone. But he did not cut his hair. Then Samson fell in love with Delilah, who was a spy for the Philistines. The sinful Philistine nation oppressed Israel and wanted to know the source of Samson's strength. Again and again Delilah asked Samson about his secret.

He lied to her twice, but finally told her the secret: if his hair was cut, he would lose his strength. Later that night, while he slept, Delilah cut Samson's hair, and his strength left him. The Philistines then attacked him, tied him up, and took him to Gaza as a prisoner. Later, as they celebrated their victory in the temple of their god, they brought Samson out to entertain them. Humiliated, Samson prayed and asked God to strengthen him one last time. Then he put his hands on the pillars of the temple. Suddenly, his strength returned and he began to push on the pillars. The building toppled and crushed everyone, including him. In death, Samson defeated more Philistines than he had in life.

THE FAITHFUL JUDGE TO COME

Despite Samson's victory over the Philistines, and despite the victories of all the previous judges over Israel's oppressors, God's people continued to reject God and worship false gods. Samson's strength could not overcome sin's grip on their hearts. But centuries later, God would send someone else to judge His people: Jesus, the righteous Judge, who would lead His people away from sin forever.

LIVING SET APART

When we trust in Jesus, we are consecrated, or set apart, from the rest of the world. Jesus sets us apart to share the gospel and to demonstrate its power to change our lives.

What are some things you do that seem strange to your friends who don't know Jesus?

Pray and ask God to help you live faithfully every day.

MEMORIZE
1 CORINTHIANS 1:9

"God is faithful; you were called by him into fellowship with his Son, Jesus Christ our Lord."

18

A FAITHFUL REEDEMER

READ THE WORD: RUTH 1-4

"May the LORD reward you for what you have done, and may you receive a full reward from the LORD God of Israel, under whose wings you have come for refuge."—Ruth 2:12

DESPERATE FOR REDEMPTION

Naomi and her family had fled to Moab to escape a famine in Israel. There, her husband died, followed by her sons, leaving only Naomi and her daughters-in-law. Naomi decided to return to Bethlehem, her hometown, and tried to send both women back to their families. One left, but the other, Ruth, refused to leave Naomi. In Bethlehem, Ruth gathered grain in a field owned by Boaz, a relative of Naomi's husband.

Boaz learned Ruth's story from one of his servants and encouraged her to stay in his fields and work. Boaz prayed that God would bless Ruth because of her faithfulness to Naomi.

Because Naomi's sons were dead, and Ruth had no children, the family's land was in danger of being lost. So, Naomi encouraged Ruth to ask Boaz to act as their "redeemer." That night, Ruth went to speak with him, and Boaz agreed to marry Ruth and redeem Naomi's property. But first, he had to speak with another relative who was closer than he to Naomi's husband. When he saw the man at the town gate, Boaz shared Ruth and Naomi's situation and asked the man if he would act as their redeemer and marry Ruth. The man refused and gave his right to Boaz, so Boaz redeemed Ruth and took her to be his wife.

THE PROMISED REDEEMER

Boaz redeemed Ruth, protecting her from harm and rescuing her from distress. Soon, they had a son, Obed. He grew up and was the father of Jesse. Jesse was the father of David, the great king of Israel, the king to whom all others would be compared. From David's family line would come another Redeemer; one greater than His ancestor Boaz, the One promised for centuries—Jesus, the Redeemer, who would give His life to rescue His bride, the church, and destroy the power of sin forever.

LIVING AS REDEEMED PEOPLE

When we trust in Jesus, we are rescued from sin and death. We are redeemed people, brought into God's family as His children.

If you believe in Jesus, how does it make you feel to know that you are part of God's family?

Pray and ask God to help you live faithfully as His child this week.

MEMORIZE TITUS 2:14

"He gave himself for us to redeem us from all lawlessness and to cleanse for himself a people for his own possession, eager to do good works."

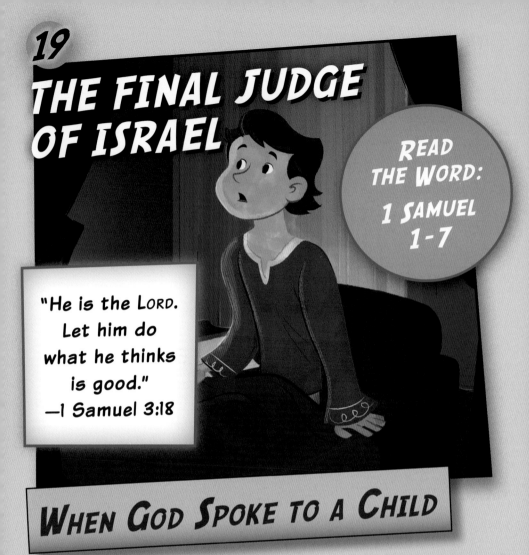

19
THE FINAL JUDGE OF ISRAEL

READ THE WORD: 1 SAMUEL 1-7

"He is the LORD. Let him do what he thinks is good."
—1 Samuel 3:18

WHEN GOD SPOKE TO A CHILD

When young Samuel heard a voice calling his name in the night, he was sure it was Eli, the high priest. Samuel had been raised by the old man, and he served in the tabernacle where God's people met with God. Twice before, the boy had heard the mysterious voice say his name, and each time, he had run to Eli. But Eli hadn't called for him. When it happened a third time, Eli realized that God must be speaking to Samuel. So he told the boy that if he heard the voice again, he was to answer, "Speak, Lord, for your servant is listening." The voice called to Samuel again, and the boy answered as Eli had instructed.

God gave Samuel a message, a warning of judgment against the high priest's family; Eli's sons were evil men. They didn't love the Lord or respect their responsibilities as priests. God told Samuel that He was going to punish them for everything they had done. When Samuel told Eli what God had said, Eli accepted God's rejection of him and his family.

As Samuel grew, he continued to serve in the tabernacle. Eventually, the prophecy about Eli's family came to pass when the Philistines attacked Israel. But the Lord was with Samuel, and after Eli's death, he took his role as the final judge of Israel.

WHEN GOD BECAME A CHILD

Samuel was just a boy when God gave him a message for the high priest. God had rejected Eli and his family because of their sins and their refusal to honor God, and He used a child to tell them so. God went a step further with the birth of Jesus by not *using* a child but by *becoming* one. As Jesus grew, the Lord was with Him. In His life, death, and resurrection, Jesus gave His perfection so that all who believe in Him would be approved by God forever.

How God Continues to Use a Child

Samuel's story reminds us that God doesn't just use adults to fulfill His plans for the world. He will use anyone for His glory, no matter how old they are.

In what ways do you think God could use you? Are you willing?

One of the things that keeps us from doing what God has commanded is the fear of rejection. Ask God to help you remember that since you've trusted in Jesus, you are approved by God forever.

MEMORIZE
1 THESSALONIANS 2:4

"Just as we have been approved by God to be entrusted with the gospel, so we speak, not to please people, but rather God, who examines our hearts."

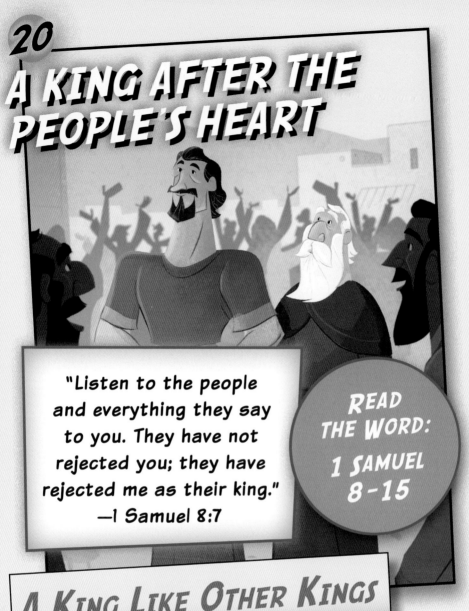

20

A KING AFTER THE PEOPLE'S HEART

"Listen to the people and everything they say to you. They have not rejected you; they have rejected me as their king."
—1 Samuel 8:7

READ THE WORD:
1 SAMUEL 8-15

A KING LIKE OTHER KINGS

When Samuel was an old man, the people of Israel demanded a king to rule over them, one like the kings of the other nations. Samuel warned them that this was a terrible idea—God was the only king they needed! But God told Samuel to do as the people wished. Their rejection of God was part of His plan. So Samuel went to find them a king.

In time, Samuel met a young Benjamite man named Saul. He looked exactly like you'd expect a king to look: tall, handsome, and strong. Samuel poured oil over Saul's head and told him the Lord had anointed him as ruler of Israel.

Saul's reign as king began well. He led Israel to victories against Moab, Edom, the kings of Zobah, and the Philistines. He rescued Israel from those who plundered them. But Saul feared people rather than God. He made an offering that only the priest was supposed to make. Then he made a rash vow that nearly cost his son's life. The final straw, though, came when Saul was commanded to destroy everything belonging to the Amalekites, but he kept the best of the livestock for himself. Saul had failed to obey God once again. There would not be another time. Saul would not continue to rule Israel. God had another king in mind for God's people.

A BETTER KIND OF KING

Saul was a king after the people's heart, one like the kings of the other nations. His reign showed why God's people needed a better King, a King who would love the Lord with all His heart, defeat His enemies, and rule faithfully. The only King they ever actually needed: Jesus, the King of kings, who never fails His people and rules from His throne forever.

GOD CARES ABOUT YOUR HEART

Saul looked like a king, but he lacked character that made him worthy to rule. Let's not be like him. God doesn't judge us by our outside appearance. He looks at our hearts and sees what we care about most.

Have you ever unfairly judged someone based on their outside appearance (what they look like, how they speak, etc.)? Go to that person and ask for forgiveness.

We've all been tempted to please people instead of obeying God. Pray that God's Spirit will help you keep Him as most important in your heart.

MEMORIZE MATTHEW 6:21

"For where your treasure is, there your heart will be also."

21

A SHEPHERD WHO SLAYED A GIANT

> "Humans do not see what the LORD sees, for humans see what is visible, but the LORD sees the heart."
> —1 Samuel 16:7

READ THE WORD: 1 SAMUEL 16-17

A VICTORY FOR GOD'S PEOPLE

Goliath, the Philistine giant, couldn't believe his eyes: a teenage boy was coming to face him on the battlefield. "*This* is Israel's champion?" he laughed. But he didn't know what David knew. Earlier, God had sent Samuel to Bethlehem to anoint the king who would replace Saul.

God told him to go to the home of Jesse, because one of his sons would be king. Samuel first saw Jesse's son Eliab. Though he was the oldest, God rejected him. The same happened with the next son, and the next, and the next. Finally, Samuel asked Jesse if he had any more sons. Jesse told him that his youngest son was out tending the sheep. Samuel said, "Send for him." As soon as Samuel saw David, the youngest son, God said, "He is the one." The Spirit of God was on David powerfully from that day forward.

This is what the giant didn't know: God was with David—and if God was with him, no one could stand against him. David rushed toward the giant, Israel's enemy, with nothing but a sling in his hand. He reached into his shoulder bag, took out a stone, and slung it at Goliath. The stone struck the giant in the forehead, and he fell to the ground, defeated.

A GREATER VICTORY TO COME

David knew he could defeat his enemy because God was with him. David's victory over Goliath turned the tide of the battle between Israel and the Philistines. When the giant fell, the Philistines were defeated! Seeing David's victory, the Israelites rushed into battle against those who remained.

David's victory offers a picture of another victory to come over an even more fearsome enemy. On the cross, Jesus defeated sin and death, the enemy oppressing God's people. Through Jesus's victory, all who trust in Him can experience victory over sin and temptation in their lives.

OUR CONFIDENCE TO LIVE FAITHFULLY

When we trust in Christ, we can be courageous in knowing that He is with us. There is no sin that cannot be overcome by His strength because He has already defeated it.

What is the biggest temptation you face? Do you believe God can help you overcome it?

It's easy to think about God helping us say no to sin. God also helps us say yes to doing what is right. Pray and ask Him to help you in both ways this week.

MEMORIZE ROMANS 8:37

"In all these things we are more than conquerors through him who loved us."

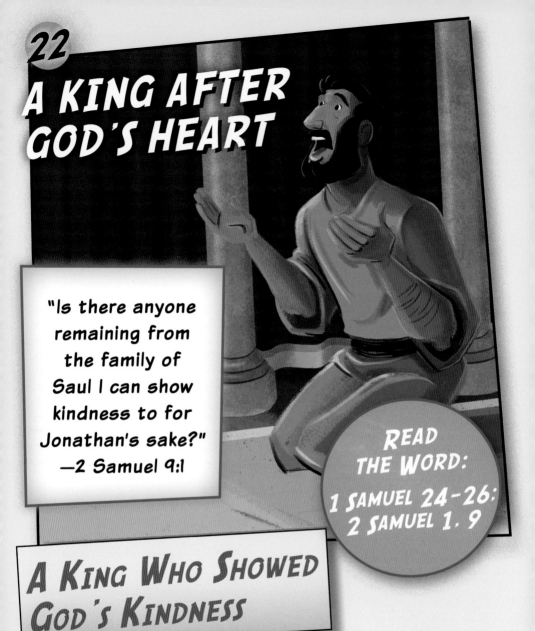

22

A KING AFTER GOD'S HEART

"Is there anyone remaining from the family of Saul I can show kindness to for Jonathan's sake?"
—2 Samuel 9:1

READ THE WORD:
1 SAMUEL 24-26;
2 SAMUEL 1. 9

A KING WHO SHOWED GOD'S KINDNESS

Jealousy is a dangerous thing, as David learned. After defeating Goliath, David became the most admired man in Israel. As David's fame grew, so did Saul's jealousy. The king plotted to kill his young rival, but because the Lord was with David, he was always spared. Even so, the attempts on his life kept coming, and finally, after David was warned by Jonathan (the king's son and David's closest friend) he fled.

David spent years as a fugitive, continually evading Saul and his men. And then the opportunity came: David and his men were hiding in a cave when Saul entered it, completely unaware of David's presence. David's men told him that the Lord was giving Saul to him. Now was his opportunity! David, however, did not attack Saul. Instead, he sneaked up behind him and cut the corner off the king's robe.

When Saul left the cave, David revealed himself and showed Saul the piece of fabric he had cut. The king admitted he had sinned against David, but his pursuit did not end. Even so, David refused to raise a hand against Saul. And when Saul and Jonathan were killed by the Philistines, David mourned for them and avenged their deaths. David continued to show mercy to Saul's family by welcoming Jonathan's son Mephibosheth into his home.

THE KINDNESS OF GOD TO US

Saul continually sinned against David, but David did not repay the king's evil with evil. Instead, David showed kindness and mercy to Saul and his family, even after Saul's death. His kindness is a picture of the kindness God shows us through Jesus. Even though we all have sinned against Him, God showed kindness to us by sending Jesus to live perfectly on our behalf and to die in our place on the cross. When we trust in Him, God shows us the greatest kindness of all and welcomes us into His family forever.

SHOWING GOD'S KINDNESS TO OTHERS

Because of the kindness God has shown to us in Jesus, we are called to show God's kindness to others.

Think about a time when someone was kind to you when you didn't deserve it. How did it make you feel?

How can you demonstrate God's kindness to someone you know today?

MEMORIZE
COLOSSIANS 3:12

"Therefore, as God's chosen ones, holy and dearly loved, put on compassion, kindness, humility, gentleness, and patience."

23

A KING WHO NEEDED A NEW HEART

"David responded to Nathan, 'I have sinned against the LORD.'"
—2 Samuel 12:13

READ THE WORD:
2 SAMUEL 11–12;
PSALM 51

A KING BROKEN BY HIS SIN

Nathan, a prophet, came to David with a problem. A rich man, he said, had many sheep. Another man was poor and had only a small lamb he loved as though it were his own child. When a traveler stayed at the rich man's home, the rich man stole the poor man's lamb to feed his guest. David was outraged when he heard Nathan's story and demanded to know who this rich man was, because he deserved to die. Nathan then replied, "You are the man!" His words cut deep into David's heart.

Nathan was right. When Israel was at war with its enemies, David had remained behind in Jerusalem. One night, he went out on his balcony and saw Bathsheba, Uriah's wife, bathing on her rooftop. He should have looked away. Instead, he had her brought to the palace. That night, David sinned against Uriah and against the Lord. Later, when Bathsheba came to David and told him she was expecting a baby, his baby, he tried to cover up his sin by sending Uriah into a fierce battle to be killed. Then David took Bathsheba as his wife, and the baby was born. No one knew David's sin—no one but God, that is. David was heartbroken when his sin was uncovered, but God forgave David's sin. Even though there would be consequences, God would not abandon him.

THE KING WHO RESTORES HIS PEOPLE

When confronted, David repented, or turned away, from his sin, and God was faithful to forgive and restore the king—promising that a Son of David would rule forever. That Son would be the One who would wash away the sin that stained David's heart, and by faith, make it new. Centuries later, the Son was revealed to be Jesus, who restores the joy of salvation to all who come to Him with humble and contrite spirits.

RESPONDING TO THE PROMISE OF RESTORATION

When we sin, there will always be consequences. But just as God did with David, God will forgive and restore us when we confess our sins—because of Jesus.

Think about a time when you sinned. What were the consequences? How did you react?

When we sin, we need to ask forgiveness from God and from the people we sin against. Who do you need to ask to forgive you?

MEMORIZE
1 JOHN 1:9

"If we confess our sins, he is faithful and righteous to forgive us our sins and to cleanse us from all unrighteousness."

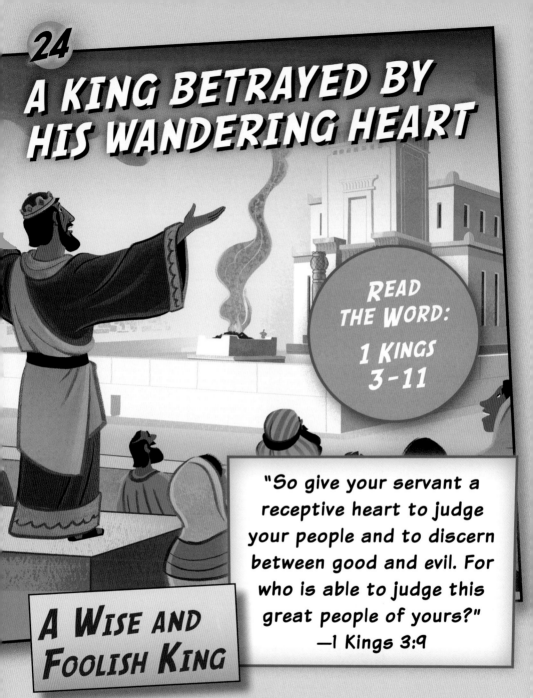

24

A KING BETRAYED BY HIS WANDERING HEART

**READ THE WORD:
1 KINGS 3-11**

"So give your servant a receptive heart to judge your people and to discern between good and evil. For who is able to judge this great people of yours?"
—1 Kings 3:9

A WISE AND FOOLISH KING

Solomon could have asked God for anything. All he desired was wisdom to rule God's people well and discern between good and evil. God was pleased with Solomon's request, and He made him wiser than any person who had ever lived. Solomon, David's son, became king after his father died.

In the beginning, Solomon ruled justly and wisely, and Israel became stronger and wealthier than it ever had been or would be again. His reputation was known throughout the world. Solomon built the temple in Jerusalem and prayed it would be a place where people from every nation would meet with God and worship Him.

For much of his rule, peace and prosperity reigned. But even the wisest man to ever live wasn't wise enough to escape the power of sin. Solomon's fortune grew. He built a palace even greater than the temple for himself. He married many women and worshiped their gods, and the nation followed him. He began to treat his workmen harshly, making demands that were too difficult for the workers. And when Solomon died, his foolishness lived on and led to the destruction of the nation.

A KING AND A KINGDOM THAT WILL NEVER FAIL

Solomon's rule started strong but ended in disaster. When Solomon was at his best, his kingdom was as close to heaven on earth as you could get. At his worst, Solomon proved that even the best of human leaders can fail. His imperfect reign points to a greater kingdom to come, one that will never end. There peace will reign forever, and a great King will be on the throne. Jesus is that King. He is not only wise; He is wisdom, and He died to make our wandering hearts true.

FOLLOWING JESUS AND LIVING WISELY

Few of us like receiving discipline, but it is a gift from God that helps increase our wisdom.

How do you respond when your parents discipline you? Why?

What in your life distracts you from following God? Ask God to give you wisdom to see those distractions for what they are and get rid of them.

MEMORIZE JAMES 1:5

"Now if any of you lacks wisdom, he should ask God—who gives to all generously and ungrudgingly— and it will be given to him."

25
THE KINGDOM DIVIDED

"What portion do we have in David? We have no inheritance in the son of Jesse. Israel, return to your tents; David, now look after your own house!"—1 Kings 12:16

THE KINGDOM SPLIT IN TWO

READ THE WORD: 1 KINGS 12-14

When Rehoboam, Solomon's son, became king, his father's workforce came to him and asked for compassion. Rehoboam asked his father's advisors what to do, and they encouraged him to show mercy. Then he turned to his own friends, who told him to treat the workers even more harshly than Solomon had. Taking his friends' foolish advice, Rehoboam threatened the workers. Jeroboam, a former servant of Solomon's, declared that Israel would not serve Rehoboam, and the nation split in two: the southern kingdom of Judah, ruled by Rehoboam, and the northern kingdom of Israel, with Jeroboam as its king.

Jeroboam feared the people would return to Rehoboam's rule if they went back to Jerusalem to worship God in the temple. So, he crafted two golden calves, and Israel began worshiping them. Rehoboam's people also began worshiping false gods, setting up altars to their idols and betraying the Lord. War raged between the two kingdoms, and as each fell further into sin, only one thing awaited: judgment.

THE PROMISE UNBROKEN

Despite the sins of Rehoboam and Jeroboam, God wasn't done with Israel. Even though they would continue to disobey Him, God would keep His covenant, the promise He had made to Abraham, Isaac, and Jacob. He would keep the vow He made to David too, that his Son would sit on the throne forever. Jesus, the descendant of David, would one day come into the world and rescue His people from their sins.

THE KING WHO RECONCILES

Sin always destroys relation- ships, but Jesus restores them. He came to reconcile people from every nation—restoring their relationship with God—and welcome them into His kingdom, one that will last forever.

When you need help making a decision, who do you talk to?

Do you have a relationship that has been hurt because of sin? Pray that God would reconcile it today.

MEMORIZE HEBREWS 1:8

"Your throne, O God, is forever and ever, and the scepter of your kingdom is a scepter of justice."

26

THE POWER OF GOD

READ THE WORD:

1 KINGS 17-19

"The God who answers with fire, he is God."
—1 Kings 18:24

A POWERFUL PROPHET

Which should the people worship: the Lord or Baal? The prophet Elijah wanted to settle this question once and for all. So he gathered all Israel together, along with the priests of their false god, Baal, and gave a challenge: whoever could make fire fall from heaven would be the true God—the only one worthy of worship. Israel agreed, and the prophets of Baal prepared an offering. They prayed. And prayed. And chanted. And prayed some more. They shouted and sang. They even cut themselves! But nothing happened. Elijah mocked them, so they tried even harder. Still, nothing happened.

Then Elijah came forward. He prepared his sacrifice then poured water all over it. Then he did it again, and again, until the offering, the firewood, and the altar were completely soaked. Elijah prayed, asking the Lord to show that He is the true God. Fire fell from heaven and consumed everything—the offering, the wood, and even the altar itself! The people were amazed. They declared that the Lord was the true God, and they worshiped Him.

A PROPHET GREATER THAN ELIJAH

When the Israelites saw the power of God at work through Elijah, they worshiped—but their worship was temporary. They continued to worship false gods and reject the Lord. Even so, Elijah's ministry was not fruitless. He pointed to another Prophet who would do even mightier works than he, one who would feed thousands, heal the sick, cleanse lepers, proclaim good news to captives, and even raise the dead! Jesus was the One Elijah pointed to, and all who trust in Him will be welcomed into His kingdom to worship Him forever.

THE POWER TO CHANGE LIVES

There are many different beliefs and religions in the world, but only one has any real power in it. The gospel changes lives because it is "the power of God for salvation to everyone who believes" (Romans 1:16).

Nothing can stop the gospel from changing someone's life. Pray for someone you know to have his or her life changed by the gospel.

How have you seen the power of the gospel at work in your life?

MEMORIZE
1 THESSALONIANS 1:4–5

"For we know, brothers and sisters loved by God, that he has chosen you, because our gospel did not come to you in word only, but also in power, in the Holy Spirit, and with full assurance."

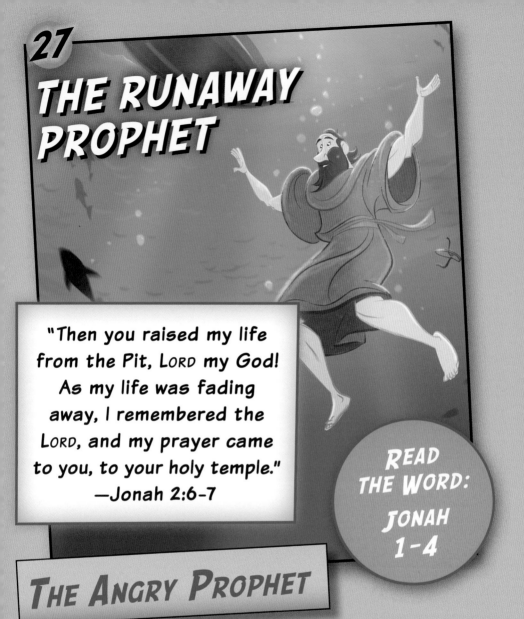

27

THE RUNAWAY PROPHET

"Then you raised my life from the Pit, LORD my God! As my life was fading away, I remembered the LORD, and my prayer came to you, to your holy temple."
—Jonah 2:6-7

READ THE WORD: JONAH 1-4

THE ANGRY PROPHET

Imagine being told to give a message to someone you despise—and if that weren't bad enough, the message was an offer of forgiveness. That was what God told Jonah to do when He sent the prophet to Nineveh. Jonah hated the Ninevites. They were cruel and evil people. He knew God's character and that if God was sending him to speak to them, He was planning to show them mercy.

In defiance, Jonah got on a boat sailing in the opposite direction. But God sent a storm to overtake the boat. When the crew tried to figure out the cause of the storm, they realized it was because of the runaway prophet. Jonah told the men to throw him overboard to stop the storm. When he hit the water, Jonah was swallowed by a great fish. After three days, the fish spit Jonah onto dry land, and God again told him to go to Nineveh.

When Jonah arrived, he proclaimed that Nineveh would be destroyed in forty days. Then he left the city and waited to see what would happen next. And what happened next infuriated him: when the people turned from their sin, praying that God would not destroy them, God showed them mercy! God asked Jonah why he was so angry. Didn't God have the right to save these people—or, for that matter, even the animals? But Jonah gave no answer.

SALVATION BELONGS TO THE LORD

When Jonah was in the belly of the fish, he remembered that salvation belongs to the Lord. God's desire was to save anyone who would turn from sin and believe in Him. He would go to any length accomplish this goal. Centuries later, God would make this clear by sending another Prophet—One who wept over a city facing judgment—who would spend three days in His own grave and be raised again. A Prophet who would proclaim the message Jonah knew to be true: salvation belongs to the Lord. That Prophet was Jesus.

THE GOOD NEWS OF GOD'S PATIENCE

God's patience can seem frustrating to us, especially when we see how much sin goes on in the world. But God's patience is good news because He wants to save all who turn from their sin and believe in Him.

Think about a time when someone you know—maybe a classmate or a sibling—seemed to get away with doing something wrong. How did that make you feel? Why?

Just as God is patient with us, He wants us to be patient with others. Ask God for the gift of patience today.

MEMORIZE 2 PETER 3:9

"The Lord does not delay his promise, as some understand delay, but is patient with you, not wanting any to perish but all to come to repentance."

28

NEW LIFE FROM A PROMISED RESCUER

"CAN THESE BONES LIVE?"

After Israel divided into two kingdoms, God's people rejected Him and worshiped false gods. But God kept pursuing them, sending prophets to speak to the people and call them to turn away from their sins. One of these prophets was a man named Ezekiel. God brought Ezekiel to a valley filled with dry bones, the bodies of soldiers who had died long ago. God asked Ezekiel if the bones could live. The prophet answered, "Lord God, only you know." God told Ezekiel to speak to the bones and say, "Get up! Put flesh on and live!" Ezekiel obeyed, and so did the bones! God sent His Spirit into them, and they became alive. These, God said, were like His people. They might look alive, but they were dead because of their sin. God was going to give life to His people and place His Spirit in them so they would live.

"Dry bones, hear the word of the LORD!"
—Ezekiel 37:4

READ THE WORD:
EZEKIEL 37:1-14

GOD'S PROMISE TO HIS PEOPLE

The vision God gave Ezekiel was a picture of something greater that God had in mind. For centuries, God had promised that a Rescuer would come to save His people. They called Him the Messiah. Each prophet gave more details about Him: He was a descendent of David. He was a king. He was God Himself. The Rescuer the people waited for was Jesus, and He made Ezekiel's vision come true. God forgives the sins of all who believe and covers them with Jesus's righteousness through their faith in Him. God puts His Spirit inside them. He gives them new hearts and new life. Jesus makes sinful people new creations (2 Corinthians 5:17) who are welcomed into God's family forever.

LIVING AS NEW CREATIONS

The Bible talks about sin in terms of life and death: sin leads to death, and faith leads to life. All who believe in Jesus are given new life, with God's Spirit living in us to help us love and please God.

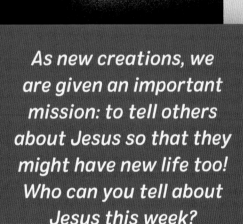

Even though people who trust Jesus are new creations, the habits of sinning can still be present in our lives. Pray that God's Spirit would help you break those habits in your life.

As new creations, we are given an important mission: to tell others about Jesus so that they might have new life too! Who can you tell about Jesus this week?

MEMORIZE
2 CORINTHIANS 5:17

"Therefore, if anyone is in Christ, he is a new creation; the old has passed away, and see, the new has come!"

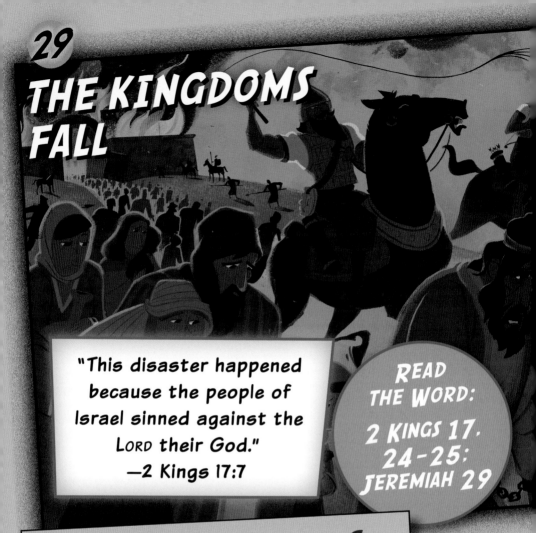

29

THE KINGDOMS FALL

"This disaster happened because the people of Israel sinned against the LORD their God."
—2 Kings 17:7

READ THE WORD:

2 KINGS 17, 24–25; JEREMIAH 29

THE CONSEQUENCES OF SIN

For more than 325 years, Israel and Judah had failed to obey the Lord. The northern kingdom of Israel only followed false gods. Each king was worse than the last. The people despised the Lord and refused to turn away from their sin. The Assyrians attacked and surrounded Samaria. After three years, the city was captured and Israel fell. The people were taken away and scattered throughout the cities of the Medes, another nation under Assyrian rule. Israel still did not repent.

The southern kingdom of Judah was no better. Although Judah had some kings who remained faithful and led the people to worship only God, the times of faithfulness did not last. Evil kings, proud and foolish, took the throne and led the people to abandon the Lord and worship false gods. One hundred fifteen years after Israel fell, Babylon surrounded Jerusalem. They sacked the temple and burned it to the ground. The palace was destroyed. The walls were broken down, and the people were led away in chains, captives of the Babylonians.

THE RESTORATION OF SINNERS

Israel and Judah fell because they did not worship the Lord. They did not care about Him or His commands. Even though they rejected Him, God was not finished with His people. He sent them a message of hope—a promise of restoration. The people would eventually return home. They would be restored when they turned back to God. This restoration, however, was merely a step toward the promise God made in the beginning. The greater restoration would come for people from every nation on earth. This restoration would put an end to sin and death so people could enjoy a relationship with God forever and ever. The restoration of sinners comes to those who call upon the name of Jesus Christ.

RESTORATION FOR ALL WHO BELIEVE

Sin always has consequences, but God promises to restore all who call to Him.

Think about a time when someone sinned against you. How did it make you feel? How do you think God feels when people continue to sin against Him?

Have you sinned against someone else? How can you make things right between the two of you?

MEMORIZE
ROMANS 6:23

"For the wages of sin is death, but the gift of God is eternal life in Christ Jesus our Lord."

30

"EVEN IF HE DOESN'T..."

READ
THE WORD:
DANIEL 1-6

"But even if he does not rescue us, we want you as king to know that we will not serve your gods or worship the gold statue you set up."—Daniel 3:18

UNCOMPROMISING FAITH

Shadrach, Meshach, and Abednego were taken into captivity when Judah fell. They did not follow the customs of the Babylonians. They refused to eat certain foods. They insisted on worshiping their own God. But their God gave them wisdom and understanding, and King Nebuchadnezzar honored them. The kings other advisors were jealous of these men (and their friend Daniel too).

The advisors fantasized about how they might get rid of them. Then the king practically handed his evil men their opportunity; he made a golden statue and commanded that everyone worship it whenever they heard music. Those who failed to do so would be killed, thrown into a fiery furnace.

When Shadrach, Meshach, and Abednego refused to bow, the evil advisors went to the king. Nebuchadnezzar ordered the three friends to worship the statue. But still they refused. They could not worship the statue because they could only worship the true God—the One who made everything. The king threw them into the fire, but as he watched to see if they had been killed, he saw something incredible: the three friends were alive and unharmed. Nebuchadnezzar commanded that they be released and then decreed that anyone who said anything offensive about their God—the true God—would be put to death.

DELIVERED THROUGH THE FIRE

When Shadrach, Meshach, and Abednego were in the fire, there was another with them, one who looked like "a son of the gods" (Daniel 3:25). God was with them in their trial and delivered them from it. Centuries later, God would do something greater. He wouldn't simply be with His people through their trial, He would walk through it on their behalf when Jesus, the Son of God, was sentenced to death and gave His life willingly as payment for sin.

STANDING FIRM IN YOUR FAITH

Just as Shadrach, Meshach, and Abednego knew they could not compromise their faith, we are called to stand firm in ours. Nothing and no one else is worthy of worship except God—the Father, Son, and Holy Spirit.

How can you show that Jesus is the only One worthy of worship this week?

Do you ever feel pressure to compromise your faith in Jesus? Write down one or two ways and pray for God to give you strength to stand firm.

MEMORIZE MARK 8:36

"For what does it benefit someone to gain the whole world and yet lose his life?"

31

"FOR SUCH A TIME AS THIS"

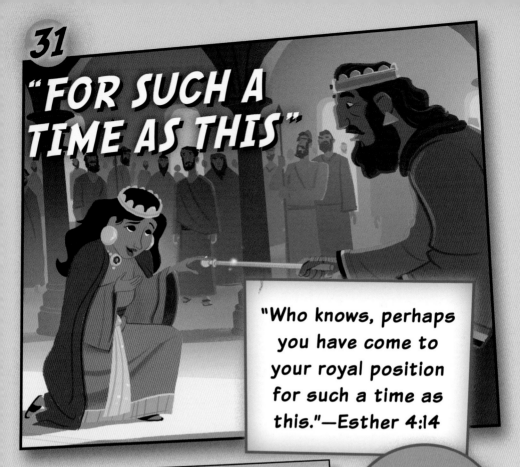

"Who knows, perhaps you have come to your royal position for such a time as this."—Esther 4:14

IN THE RIGHT PLACE AT THE RIGHT TIME

READ THE WORD: ESTHER 1-10

What if you had the power to stop a terrible crime from happening but to use that power would put you in terrible danger? You'd probably know what it felt like to be Esther, the Jewish queen of King Ahasuerus's empire. One of the king's advisors, an evil man named Haman, hated the Jews—the people of Judah scattered throughout the Persian Empire—because Mordecai, the man who had raised Esther, refused to bow down to him. Furious, Haman planned to have not just Mordecai but all the Jews killed.

He sent orders to every corner of the kingdom. When Mordecai discovered Haman's plot, he begged Esther to speak to the king. Perhaps this was why she was the queen in the first place, he said.

When Esther arrived in the king's court, Ahasuerus welcomed Esther and asked what he could do for her. She invited both the king and Haman to a banquet she had prepared. At the banquet, the king asked again what he could do for her. Esther invited both men to another banquet the next night, where she revealed that someone was plotting to kill her people: Haman! Now the king was furious! He executed Haman and sent orders allowing the Jews to defend themselves against anyone who attacked them. The Jews overpowered all who attacked them. Victorious, they celebrated, and Mordecai became the second in command of Ahasuerus's kingdom.

Another Rescuer, At Just the Right Time

God didn't speak a single word in Esther's story. In fact, He isn't even mentioned in it. But He was at work the whole time, using all things according to His purposes (Romans 8:28) and seeking the good of His people. It was this way from the very beginning. Throughout history, God has used all things, good and bad, to bring about His plan to rescue and redeem people from every nation through the life, death, and resurrection of Jesus Christ.

TRUSTING THAT GOD IS AT WORK

Sometimes it's hard to believe God cares about us, especially when we feel helpless or afraid. But even though we may not always be aware of God working, we can trust He *is* always at work to bring about His plans.

Is it hard to believe that God is always at work? Why?

Why can we have confidence that God's plans will come true?

MEMORIZE ROMANS 5:6

"For while we were still helpless, at the right time, Christ died for the ungodly."

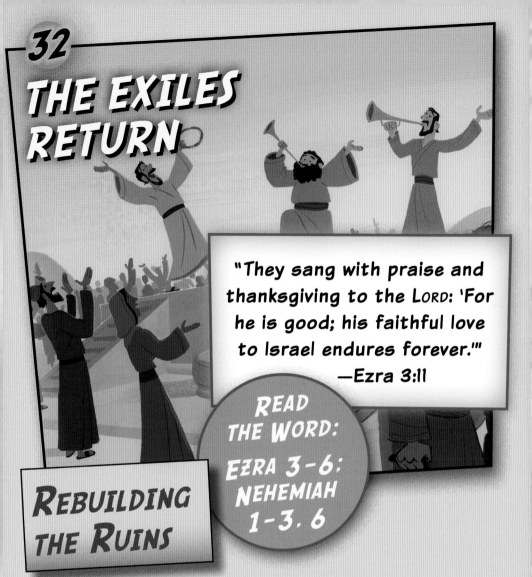

32

THE EXILES RETURN

> "They sang with praise and thanksgiving to the LORD: 'For he is good; his faithful love to Israel endures forever.'"
> —Ezra 3:11

READ THE WORD: EZRA 3-6; NEHEMIAH 1-3, 6

REBUILDING THE RUINS

When God's people had been in exile for seventy years, King Cyrus of Persia issued a decree: any of the Hebrew people who wished to return to their land were free to do so. But when they arrived in Jerusalem, they had much work to do. The temple was in ruins. The city walls were destroyed. They had to rebuild. The first exiles returned and began to rebuild the temple. When the foundation was laid, many people rejoiced, but the oldest of them, the ones who remembered the first, more elaborate temple, wept.

138

The enemies of the Jews opposed the building campaign by sending letters, bribing officials, and threatening the Jews. Cyrus ordered the construction to stop. For more than ten years, the temple remained unfinished until construction resumed when Darius was king. But there was still more to do. Nehemiah, the cupbearer of King Artaxerxes, learned that Jerusalem's walls were still in ruins, and he asked the king to allow him to rebuild them. The king agreed and gave Nehemiah the supplies he needed. Despite opposition from neighboring nations, the people completed the work on Jerusalem's walls in only fifty-two days.

RESTORING THE PEOPLE

Rebuilding the city wasn't the only problem the exiles faced. The people needed to be restored. They had forgotten the Law of God. They were still subjects of other nations. There was no king on Israel's throne. But God reminded them of His promise: that the Son of David would one day sit on the throne, and His kingdom would never end. More than that, this Son of David would be the Rescuer that God promised from the beginning. He would be the Lord Himself, and He was coming to restore His people by rescuing them from their sins.

REMAINING FAITHFUL WHILE WE WAIT

Just as God's people awaited Jesus's first coming, we await His return, when He will make all things new (Revelation 21:5). God calls us to live faithfully while we wait and not to lose hope.

Do you find it hard to wait for something really amazing? Why?

Think back to all the ways you've read that God kept His promises to His people in the Bible. How can those promises encourage you today?

MEMORIZE 1 JOHN 2:28

"So now, little children, remain in him so that when he appears we may have confidence and not be ashamed before him at his coming."

33

GOD BREAKS HIS SILENCE

"The angel answered him, 'I am Gabriel, who stands in the presence of God, and I was sent to speak to you and tell you this good news.'"–Luke 1:19

READ THE WORD:

LUKE 1; MATTHEW 1

AN ANGEL APPEARS IN THE TEMPLE

God was silent for four hundred years. Totally silent. God's people waited for Him to fulfill His promise that the Messiah, the Rescuer, was coming. But when?

One night, while an elderly priest named Zechariah served in the temple, the answer came when an angel appeared. "Do not be afraid, Zechariah," the angel said. "because your prayer has been heard. Your wife Elizabeth will bear you a son, and you will name him John."

Zechariah and Elizabeth had long wanted children, but in all their years of marriage, no children came. Still, even in their old age, they had prayed, hoping God would bless them. But could it really happen now? Zechariah couldn't believe it. The angel said that because Zechariah didn't believe, he would be silent until his son was born. Zechariah left the temple, unable to speak, and went home. His wife became pregnant, and when the time came to give birth, she had a son. Her neighbors rejoiced. They wanted her to call him Zechariah, like his father, but Elizabeth said, "No. He will be called John." Everyone was confused. No one in their family had that name. So they turned to Zechariah. He took a tablet and wrote, "His name is John." Immediately, Zechariah's mouth opened and he began to speak, praising God, and everyone was amazed.

His name
is John.

Preparing the Way
for the Rescuer

When the angel spoke to Zechariah, he said that John would be filled with the Holy Spirit from the womb, and he would go out in the spirit and power of Elijah. But John was not the Messiah. He was not the promised Rescuer. John was the one promised to come before the Messiah (Malachi 3:1), who would "turn the hearts of fathers to their children, and the disobedient to the understanding of the righteous, to make ready for the Lord a prepared people" (Luke 1:17). John's birth was good news because it meant that Jesus was coming. And when Jesus came, God was going to rescue His people from their sin forever.

EMPOWERED FOR MISSION

The Holy Spirit that filled John is the same Spirit that fills everyone who believes in Jesus today. The Holy Spirit gives power to fulfill our calling to make disciples of all nations as we share the good news of the gospel.

How do you think the Jews felt during the four hundred years when God was silent? Why?

Do you feel prepared to share the gospel with others? God has given you His Spirit. Pray and ask Him to help you as you tell others about Jesus.

MEMORIZE
2 CORINTHIANS 1:20

"For every one of God's promises is 'Yes' in him. Therefore, through him we also say 'Amen' to the glory of God."

34

GOOD NEWS OF GREAT JOY

READ THE WORD:
LUKE 1-2; MATTHEW 2

THE FAVORED ONE OF GOD

"See, the virgin will become pregnant and give birth to a son, and they will name him Immanuel."
—Matthew 1:23

Mary couldn't believe what she was hearing. She was a young girl, hardly the sort of person to be the mother of the promised Rescuer. Yet Gabriel, an angel of the Lord, told her this would happen. She would have a Child by the Holy Spirit. She was to name Him Jesus. When she told Joseph, the man she was to marry, he had an even harder time believing it. His doubts were removed when Gabriel appeared to him as well. Months passed, and soon it was time for the baby to be born.

But Mary and Joseph had to travel to Bethlehem, the home of King David, to be counted in a census. It was during this journey that the Child was born—in a stable, surrounded by animals because there were no guest rooms available. His mother wrapped Him in swaddling cloths, and she and Joseph named Him Jesus, just as Gabriel said.

IMMANUEL, GOD WITH US

The night Jesus was born was unlike any other night in history. At the same time that Mary wrapped her Child, a group of shepherds stood amazed. An angel appeared to them and announced good news of great joy for the whole world—the Messiah, the promised Rescuer, was born. He was the One God had promised from the very beginning, the One who would crush the serpent's head and sit on David's throne. Immanuel, "God with us." Jesus, the God who saves, was born.

GIVE GLORY TO GOD

When the angels announced Jesus's birth, they gave glory to God; they worshiped. When the shepherds found Mary and Joseph, they did the same. When we meet Jesus, God wants us to worship as well. His birth is good news for us today, because only Jesus saves.

Imagine being one of the shepherds who saw the angels singing. How would you have felt? Why?

The good news of Jesus's coming to save sinners is news we are called to share with others. Who can you share it with this week?

MEMORIZE LUKE 1:32

"He will be great and will be called the Son of the Most High, and the Lord God will give him the throne of his father David."

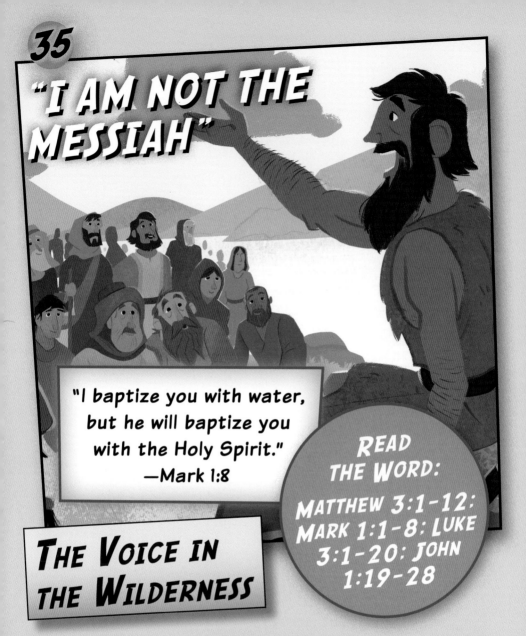

35

"I AM NOT THE MESSIAH"

"I baptize you with water, but he will baptize you with the Holy Spirit."
—Mark 1:8

READ THE WORD:
MATTHEW 3:1-12; MARK 1:1-8; LUKE 3:1-20; JOHN 1:19-28

THE VOICE IN THE WILDERNESS

People from all over Judea flocked to the wilderness, near the Jordan River. Now a grown man, John was there wearing a camel-hair tunic and a leather belt—the clothing of a prophet. John called the people to turn away from their sins and be baptized to show their need and desire for God's forgiveness. Those troubled by their sin came to him, but so did the religious leaders. When John saw them, he called them a "brood of vipers" (Matthew 3:7).

Like poisonous snakes, they poisoned people with the lie that they could earn God's forgiveness and favor through their actions. But those leaders couldn't be good enough to earn forgiveness either! Instead, John told them that God was ready to cut down the "tree" of Israel because "every tree that doesn't produce good fruit will be cut down and thrown into the fire" (Matthew 3:10). The more John preached, the more amazed people were. They wondered if he might be the promised Rescuer, the Messiah, who would restore the kingdom.

THE ONE GREATER THAN JOHN

John was not the Messiah. He was the one who prepared the way for Him. John told the people that the Rescuer was more powerful. "I baptize you with water," John said, "but he will baptize you with the Holy Spirit" (Mark 1:8). Jesus, the promised Rescuer, is more powerful than John because He is the Lord Himself. When Jesus came, He showed the people what God expected of them by living a perfect life. After His death and resurrection, Jesus sent the Holy Spirit to dwell within all who trust in Him.

PRODUCING GOOD FRUIT

John said we should "produce fruit consistent with repentance" (Matthew 3:8), which means we are supposed to obey God's commands. But we don't obey so that God *will* forgive us. We obey because He *already* has forgiven us through faith in Jesus.

It's easy to get the relationship between faith and obedience confused. Why does it matter that faith comes first?

Pray and ask God to help you obey Him. If you haven't trusted Jesus, pray that God would forgive your sins because Jesus lived, died, and was raised again for you.

MEMORIZE EPHESIANS 1:13

"In him you also were sealed with the promised Holy Spirit when you heard the word of truth, the gospel of your salvation, and when you believed."

36

JESUS'S BAPTISM AND TEMPTATION

"And a voice from heaven said: 'This is my beloved Son, with whom I am well-pleased.'"
—Matthew 3:17

READ THE WORD:
MATTHEW 3:13-4:11;
LUKE 4:1-13

THE WAY TO FULFILL ALL RIGHTEOUSNESS

John was baptizing and preaching by the Jordan River when Jesus walked toward him and asked to be baptized. Jesus didn't need to be baptized; baptism was a symbol of repentance, of turning away from sin. But Jesus never sinned. John was confused, but Jesus told him that His baptism was the way to fulfill God's plan. So John baptized Jesus, and when Jesus came up from the water, the Spirit of God came down in the form of a dove and rested on Him. Then a voice spoke and said, "This is my beloved Son, with whom I am well-pleased."

Afterward, Jesus went into the wilderness to be tempted by the devil. He didn't eat for forty days. Three times, the devil tempted Jesus: First, to turn stones to bread so He could eat. Second, to jump off the top of the temple and show that God would protect Him. And third, to worship the devil in exchange for all the kingdoms of the world. But every time, Jesus refused. It was better that He remain hungry and obey God's Word. He would not put God to the test; and only God is worthy of worship. The devil left immediately, and Jesus began His ministry.

A Savior Like— and Unlike—Us

Jesus was baptized and tempted because He was a human being. He had to keep God's commands, and it was possible for Him to be tempted, just like we are. But unlike us, He resisted every temptation. He always kept God's commands. When we trust in Jesus, God sees us in light of His righteousness—His perfection—declaring us His beloved children, with whom He is well-pleased.

TURN TO THE SAVIOR WHO UNDERSTANDS US

Jesus was tempted in all the ways we are tempted, but He did not sin (Hebrews 4:15). He knows what it's like for us, and because of that, we can turn to Him for help and forgiveness.

How does knowing that Jesus was tempted help you when you're tempted to disobey God?

How are you tempted to sin? Pray and ask Jesus to help you resist temptation.

MEMORIZE HEBREWS 4:15

"For we do not have a high priest who is unable to sympathize with our weaknesses, but one who has been tempted in every way as we are, yet without sin."

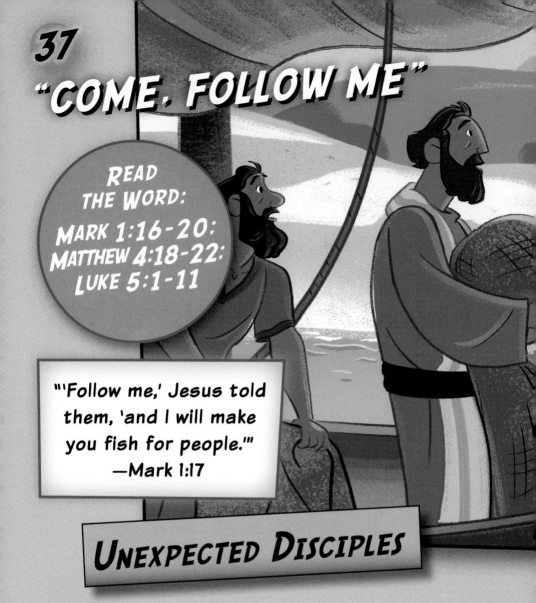

37

"COME, FOLLOW ME"

READ
THE WORD:
MARK 1:16-20;
MATTHEW 4:18-22;
LUKE 5:1-11

"'Follow me,' Jesus told them, 'and I will make you fish for people.'"
—Mark 1:17

UNEXPECTED DISCIPLES

What kind of person would you expect Jesus to call as His disciples? Maybe people who were well educated and had dedicated their lives to obeying God's commands—people like the Pharisees and other religious leaders of Judea. But Jesus did something unexpected: As He walked along the sea of Galilee, He saw Simon Peter and Andrew, two brothers, throwing a net from their fishing boat. "Come, follow Me!" He called to them. The brothers were amazed and immediately jumped out of the boat and swam to the shore.

Then Jesus called to two more fishermen, James and John, the sons of Zebedee. They also dropped their nets and went with Jesus. Then came Philip, Bartholomew, and Thomas. Then Jesus met a tax collector named Matthew and called him too. Then He called James, Thaddeus, Simon the Zealot, and finally Judas Iscariot, the one who would betray Him. These were the first of Jesus's disciples, the twelve apostles.

An Extraordinary Savior for Ordinary People

Jesus's disciples were not the kind of people anyone would expect a rabbi to call as His disciples, let alone one who was as popular as Jesus was becoming. They were not among the elite or highly educated. Some of them were even considered to be among the worst sort of sinners. They were ordinary people, the kind of people Jesus Himself came to save. But God used them to spread the gospel throughout the entire world.

FULFILL HIS PURPOSES

Just as Jesus called ordinary and unexpected people to fulfill His purposes then, He still does it today—with you! If you trust Jesus, He wants to use you to share the gospel with the world.

How does it make you feel to know that the original disciples were ordinary people like you? Why?

Do you ever feel unprepared to tell people about Jesus? Pray and ask God to help you.

MEMORIZE
1 CORINTHIANS 1:28

"God has chosen what is insignificant and despised in the world—what is viewed as nothing—to bring to nothing what is viewed as something."

38

A TEACHER WITH AUTHORITY

"He was teaching them like one who had authority, and not like their scribes."
—Matthew 7:29

READ THE WORD:
MATTHEW 5-7;
LUKE 4;
JOHN 6

ASTONISHED BY HIS TEACHING

Jesus was the most incredible teacher the Jews had ever heard. When He spoke, He didn't just say the same things other teachers said. He spoke with an authority no other teacher had. Everyone who heard Jesus was amazed as He taught about what life in God's kingdom would be like and what God expected of His people.

He spoke about how to pray and how to give. He warned His listeners about the dangers of outward obedience to God's commands while breaking those commands in their hearts. He warned of the dangers of being consumed by the cares of the world while ignoring God's kingdom. Everywhere Jesus went, people followed Him, astonished by His words.

OVERWHELMED BY THEIR UNBELIEF

Even though Jesus amazed many with His authority, He angered just as many others when He talked about what that authority really meant. When Jesus told the members of a synagogue in Nazareth that He was the Messiah, the people doubted. He warned them not to follow in the footsteps of their idol-worshipping ancestors, and they were furious. They tried to throw Jesus off a cliff. Later, when a large crowd came to Jesus, looking for food to eat, He told them that He was the bread of life and that no one who came to Him would be hungry again. But the people could not accept this, and many refused to follow Jesus any longer.

THE FOUNDATION OF YOUR LIFE

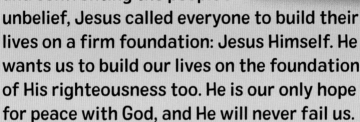

By teaching with authority and confronting the people's unbelief, Jesus called everyone to build their lives on a firm foundation: Jesus Himself. He wants us to build our lives on the foundation of His righteousness too. He is our only hope for peace with God, and He will never fail us.

Which of Jesus's teachings is most difficult for you to obey? Why?

Think about one person you know who struggles to accept what Jesus says about Himself. Pray that person would see the truth and begin to trust Jesus.

MEMORIZE
PSALM 71:5

"For you are my hope, Lord GOD, my confidence from my youth."

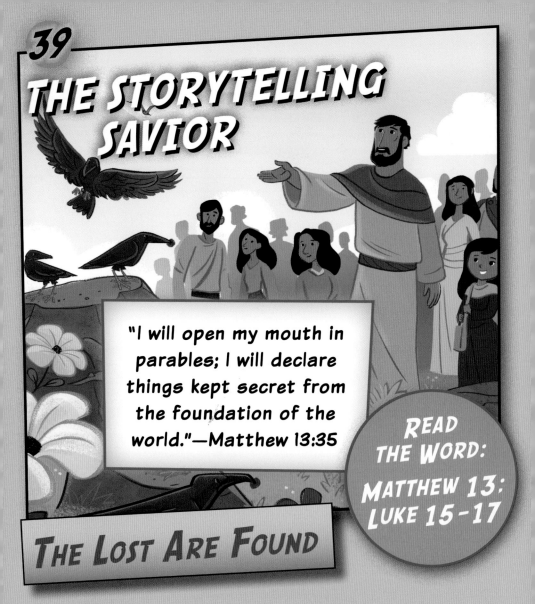

39

THE STORYTELLING SAVIOR

"I will open my mouth in parables; I will declare things kept secret from the foundation of the world."—Matthew 13:35

READ THE WORD:
MATTHEW 13; LUKE 15–17

THE LOST ARE FOUND

Throughout His ministry, Jesus taught people important truths about God and His kingdom. He wanted them to know what the kingdom is like and what it means to live as its citizens. To help people understand these truths, Jesus often taught through parables, or stories. Some of these parables were about the value of the kingdom. Others were about the good things that happen when the gospel is shared. All the parables challenged the attitudes of the people who heard them.

Among the best known parables is the story of two sons, one obedient and one rebellious. The younger son demanded his inheritance from his father. When the son received it, he spent it on wild living until nothing was left. When he realized how foolish he had been, he returned home to his father, intending to ask to be hired as a servant. But when his father saw him, he ran to his son. The father welcomed him home with joy and announced a great celebration in honor of the one who was lost but was now found. But the older brother, who had remained at home and worked in the fields, refused to celebrate his brother's return. The story ended with only a question for Jesus's hearers: will you celebrate that the lost are being found?

THE SEARCHING SHEPHERD

Not everyone heard Jesus's parables and rejoiced with Him. Some, like the religious leaders, were furious about the stories and Jesus's ministry. Like the older son, they rejected what the Father was doing and would not rejoice when the lost were found. They believed their efforts to obey God's commands were what gave them God's approval. Jesus challenged that belief because He wanted them to see they were putting their trust in the wrong thing. Rule keeping couldn't save them. But through His life, death, and resurrection, Jesus did what rule keeping could never do: He made the way for all who believe in Him to be welcomed into God's family forever.

REJOICING WITH ALL OF HEAVEN

Jesus rejoices when the lost are found. All of heaven does too. If we are part of Jesus's family, we are encouraged to do the same as God uses us to share the good news about Jesus.

Talk to your family members about how they came to know Jesus. Pray and thank God that Jesus saved them and that you get to celebrate that together.

Read a few of Jesus's parables. Which ones are most challenging to you? Why?

MEMORIZE EPHESIANS 1:9

"He made known to us the mystery of his will, according to his good pleasure that he purposed in Christ."

40

THE WONDER-WORKING GOD

"As a result, they were all astounded and gave glory to God, saying, 'We have never seen anything like this!'"—Mark 2:12

READ THE WORD:
MATTHEW 9; MARK 2; LUKE 9; JOHN 6, 11

"WHO IS THIS MAN?"

What would you do if you saw a miracle? I'm not talking about an illusion or a trick, but something that is so unexplainable you can only call it miraculous. You might be as astonished as the crowds that gathered to hear Jesus teach. They knew He was unlike any other teacher the Jews had ever seen. But it wasn't just Jesus's teaching that amazed them. Throughout His ministry, Jesus did things that shouldn't have been possible. He performed miracles.

Everywhere Jesus went, people came asking for His help, and He gladly gave it. He healed the blind, the lame, and the sick. He cured ten lepers. He healed a woman with an illness that made her bleed for more than twelve years. He made a paralyzed man walk (and forgave his sins too!). He fed people—over five thousand men, plus women and children—with only a small amount of food. He even raised His friend Lazarus from the dead! Wherever Jesus went, as He taught and performed miracles, the people asked, "Who is this man?"

THE ONE GOD'S PEOPLE WAITED FOR

In every sign and wonder, Jesus was revealing Himself to be the One God's people had waited centuries for. Jesus was the Messiah, the promised Rescuer. When Jesus displayed His power, He was telling the people that deliverance was coming. Rescue was at hand. And it would come as Jesus demonstrated His power in the most incredible way possible—the way that would bring God the most glory: by dying and rising from the dead.

STOP AND STAND AMAZED

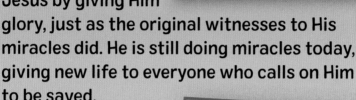

We should respond to the miracles of Jesus by giving Him glory, just as the original witnesses to His miracles did. He is still doing miracles today, giving new life to everyone who calls on Him to be saved.

Imagine you were there to witness Jesus's miracles. What would have been your reaction?

Who do you know who needs to experience the miracle of salvation today? Pray for them right now, that they will see that need for themselves.

MEMORIZE PSALM 66:5

"Come and see the wonders of God; his acts for humanity are awe-inspiring."

41

RULER OF ALL CREATION

"And they were terrified and asked one another, 'Who then is this? Even the wind and the sea obey him!'"—Mark 4:41

"WHAT KIND OF MAN IS THIS?"

READ THE WORD:

MATTHEW 8:23–34; MARK 1:21–28; 4:35–41; 5:1–20; LUKE 8:26–39

It was the worst kind of night to be in a boat. The waves were crashing, the rain was pouring, and the wind was howling. It was every experienced sailor's worst nightmare. And what was Jesus doing through it all? Sleeping. The disciples couldn't believe it! They cried out to Him, "We're going to die! Don't you care?" So Jesus got up, looked out at the storm, and simply said, "Stop."

And suddenly, it was quiet; the water was as smooth as glass. The disciples were terrified and asked, "What kind of man is this that even the winds and the waves obey Him?"

It wasn't just the winds and the waves that obeyed Jesus. Unclean, or evil, spirits did as well. When Jesus was teaching in Capernaum, a man with an evil spirit appeared in the synagogue. The spirit inside the man asked if Jesus was there to destroy him. Jesus cast the spirit out of the man. When Jesus approached another man who was tormented by evil spirits, the spirits in the man begged Jesus not to torment *them*.

Jesus cast the spirits into a herd of pigs. Everywhere He went, Jesus cast out spirits that tormented men, women, and children. And all who saw it happen were amazed by Jesus, the Man whom unclean spirits obeyed.

"I KNOW WHO YOU ARE!"

By displaying His authority over nature and unclean spirits, Jesus was showing that He was the ruler of all creation. Everything was made by Him and through Him (Colossians 1:16). The evil spirits knew this. Despite their rebellion against Him, Jesus ruled over them. They knew a day was coming when Jesus, the Son of the Most High, the Holy One of God, would sit on His throne and destroy them forever—on the day of judgment, when Jesus will make all things new.

PUT YOUR HOPE IN HIM

Jesus is in control of all things—even evil is under His authority. Although it's hard to remember, we can live in this world with hope because, by faith, we belong to the One who is the ruler of all.

Is it easy to believe Jesus is in control of all things? Why or why not?

What are you most afraid of? How can knowing that Jesus is the ruler of everything help you overcome that fear?

MEMORIZE
COLOSSIANS 2:9–10

"For the entire fullness of God's nature dwells bodily in Christ, and you have been filled by him, who is the head over every ruler and authority."

42

JESUS'S TRIUMPHAL ENTRY

READ THE WORD:
MATTHEW 21–22; LUKE 19:28– 22:6

"Hosanna to the Son of David! Blessed is he who comes in the name of the Lord! Hosanna in the highest heaven!"
—Matthew 21:9

THE SON OF DAVID ARRIVES

When Jesus entered Jerusalem, all the people rejoiced. Normally, whenever Jesus went anywhere, people were excited. They were amazed by His teaching and His miracles. But this time was special: Jesus came into the city riding a young donkey, His disciples laid their cloaks and leafy branches along the ground. It was the arrival of a King—the Son of David, the promised Rescuer, had come!

The religious leaders immediately came to Jesus and told Him to quiet the people. Jesus, however, told them that if the people stopped, the stones would cry out.

He went to the temple to teach in the court-yards. Each day He taught about the kingdom of God, and the religious leaders tried to trap Him with their questions. But every time He answered, Jesus revealed that the Pharisees did not under-stand the Scriptures. They did not know who He truly was. Furious, they were determined to kill Him. They knew they couldn't arrest Him immediately. Jesus was too popular. If they moved against Him, there would be a riot. Instead, they received an unexpected visitor: Judas Iscariot, one of Jesus's own disciples. Judas would give them Jesus when the time was right. All they had to do was wait.

PLOTS, PLANS, AND GOD'S GLORY

Even as the religious leaders and Judas plotted against Jesus, God was at work to fulfill His plans. For at least a year, from the time Peter confessed that Jesus was the Messiah, Jesus taught His disciples that He would go to Jerusalem, be handed over to the religious leaders, and be killed. The disciples didn't understand how this could be. The Messiah was supposed to be a triumphant King. But this was God's plan from the very beginning: Jesus was the promised Rescuer, but His kingdom wouldn't come by overthrowing the Roman Empire. His kingdom would come in a way no one expected—through His death. He would overthrow a greater oppressor than any human government. He would defeat sin and death. The disciples didn't know that. But soon they would.

PRAISE THE KING FOREVER

Jesus's kingdom is here in part but not in full. When He returns, the kingdom will come in full as all things are made new. While we wait, we can praise Jesus, just as we will forever on that day.

Does it seem strange that the religious leaders didn't understand that Jesus was the Messiah? Why?

Praising Jesus includes how we use our words and our actions. How can you praise Him today?

MEMORIZE ROMANS 12:1

"Therefore, brothers and sisters, in view of the mercies of God, I urge you to present your bodies as a living sacrifice, holy and pleasing to God; this is your true worship."

43

A LAMB LED TO THE SLAUGHTER

READ THE WORD:
MATTHEW 26–27;
LUKE 22:7–
23:31

"What has this man done wrong? I have found in him no grounds for the death penalty."
—Luke 23:22

THE TIME HAD COME

In all the ways we think of Jesus, it's almost impossible to think of Him being distressed or anxious. But in the garden of Gethsemane, Jesus was distressed. This would be the night He would be handed over to the religious leaders. As He ate the Passover meal with His disciples, Jesus broke bread and passed a cup around, telling them that the bread and wine were His body and blood, broken and shed for them.

Now in the garden, He prayed, "Let this cup pass from me. Yet not as I will, but as you will" (Matthew 26:39). In other words, "Your will be done, Father."

Soon, a mob arrived with swords and clubs in hand, along with the religious leaders. Leading them was Judas Iscariot. Jesus was arrested and taken away. He was put on trial and accused of blasphemy. The high priest asked if Jesus was the Son of God. Jesus answered without hesitation, as clearly as possible, "You say so" (Luke 23:3). Jesus was the Son of Man, the Son of God, the One seen in the visions of the prophets. Enraged, the high priest had Him taken away, and soon Jesus was condemned to die.

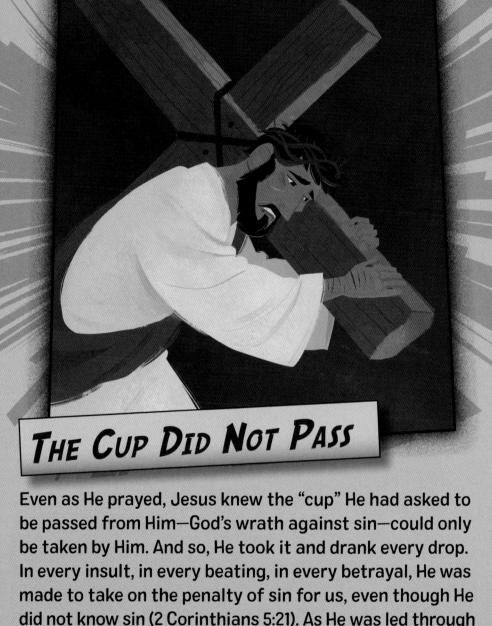

THE CUP DID NOT PASS

Even as He prayed, Jesus knew the "cup" He had asked to be passed from Him—God's wrath against sin—could only be taken by Him. And so, He took it and drank every drop. In every insult, in every beating, in every betrayal, He was made to take on the penalty of sin for us, even though He did not know sin (2 Corinthians 5:21). As He was led through the streets, carrying His own wooden cross, it was as a lamb led to the slaughter. When the nails were driven through His hands and feet, the "cup" was emptied. He was, as John the Baptist said years before, the Lamb of God, who would take away the sins of the world (John 1:29).

WE ARE HEALED THROUGH HIM

It's strange to think about Jesus's death as good news. He didn't deserve to die. He never did anything wrong. But through His death, we are healed of our sin sickness. We are given His righteousness and are welcomed into God's presence as Jesus's friends forever.

What's the hardest thing for you when reading the story of Jesus's arrest and crucifixion?

How can you live differently today because of Jesus's sacrifice?

MEMORIZE
2 CORINTHIANS 5:21

"He made the one who did not know sin to be sin for us, so that in him we might become the righteousness of God."

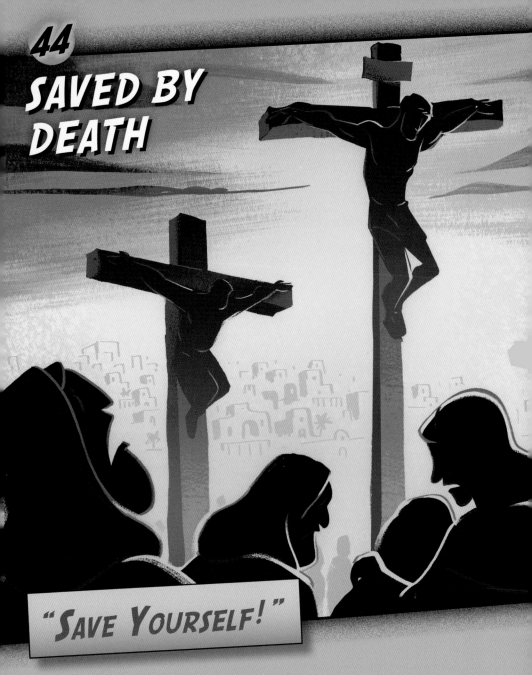

44
SAVED BY DEATH

"SAVE YOURSELF!"

It was the worst day in all of history. Jesus hung on the cross, listening as the crowd below mocked Him, saying that if He was the king of the Jews, He should come down from His cross. But He would not. He could not. His work was not finished. Instead, He prayed, "Father, forgive them because they do not know what they are doing."

READ
THE WORD:
MATTHEW 27:32-66;
LUKE 23:32-56

"And Jesus called out with a loud voice, 'Father, into your hands I entrust my spirit.'"
—Luke 23:46

At noon that day, the sky became as dark as night. At around three in the afternoon, the sun returned, and the earth shook violently. Then Jesus cried out: "It is finished" (John 19:30). *What did this mean?* the crowd wondered. *What was finished?* Jesus did not tell them. Instead, with the last of His strength, He spoke again to His Father and said, "Father, into your hands I entrust my spirit." And then He died, and as He did, the curtain in the temple split in two and revealed the most holy place.

It Is Finished

Jesus, the Son of God, was dead. His body was taken down from the cross. His disciples wrapped His body in linen cloths and placed Him in a newly cut tomb. A stone was rolled in front, and it was sealed. Guards stood outside its entrance in case anyone tried to steal His body and claim that He had come back from the dead. But the worst day in history was also one of the best days in history. Jesus's work was complete. The payment for sin had been made. He had willingly laid down His life, "so that everyone who believes in him will not perish but have eternal life" (John 3:16). Jesus was dead. Soon He was going to take up His life again.

HUMBLED BY OUR RESCUE

God paid a great price to rescue sinners—the death of His only Son. We should be humbled by this and give thanks that we can enjoy a relationship with God forever because of what Jesus did on the cross. Punishment for sin is finished in Jesus for all who trust in Him.

Why is Jesus's death called "good news"?

Think about how you've sinned, either doing something wrong or failing to do what was right. Thank God that these sins were paid for by Jesus on the cross, and ask Him to help you live faithfully.

MEMORIZE ROMANS 3:23–24

"For all have sinned and fall short of the glory of God. They are justified freely by his grace through the redemption that is in Christ Jesus."

45

JESUS IS ALIVE!

"Weren't our hearts burning within us while he was talking with us on the road and explaining the Scriptures to us?"
—Luke 24:32

READ THE WORD: MATTHEW 28: LUKE 24: JOHN 20-21

THE EMPTY TOMB AND THE EMMAUS ROAD

What if the thing you most hoped for actually happened but you didn't realize it? That was the experience of two of Jesus's disciples as they walked from Jerusalem to Emmaus after the Passover. Jesus, the one they thought was the Messiah, was dead. His body was laid in a tomb. Guards were posted at the entrance of the tomb, and a stone was rolled in front of it. But some of the women who had followed Jesus came to the disciples with strange news: the tomb was empty. His body was gone, and an angel had appeared and said that Jesus was alive! Could it be true?

As the two men walked along, Jesus joined them, but they didn't recognize Him. Jesus asked what they were talking about. When the disciples told Him, Jesus said, "Didn't you know this was supposed to happen—that the Messiah had to suffer these things and enter into His glory?" Then, beginning with Moses and all the Prophets, Jesus taught them all the things about Himself from the Scriptures. Later, the men invited Jesus to share a meal with them. As He gave thanks and broke the bread, they recognized Him—and then He disappeared. But the two men knew the exciting truth—Jesus was alive! They raced back to Jerusalem, eager to tell the other disciples the good news.

SIN AND DEATH ARE DEFEATED

For forty days after His resurrection, Jesus kept appearing to His disciples. He ate with them. He invited Thomas to touch the wounds in His hands. He restored Peter after His denial of Jesus. He even appeared to as many as five hundred people at one time. Jesus, the Messiah, the promised Rescuer, was alive—and is still alive! He defeated death, and His resurrection is only part of the plan. When He returns to make all things new, all who believe in Him will be resurrected to enjoy life with Jesus forever.

TELL THE GOOD NEWS OF THE RISEN CHRIST

While we wait for Jesus's return, we are called to share the same message as the Emmaus disciples with everyone we know: Jesus is alive!

Is it hard for you to believe the resurrection happened? Why?

Many people doubt that the resurrection of Jesus actually happened. Pray that God would help them see the truth and believe that Jesus defeated sin and death for them.

MEMORIZE LUKE 24:27

"Then beginning with Moses and all the Prophets, he interpreted for them the things concerning himself in all the Scriptures."

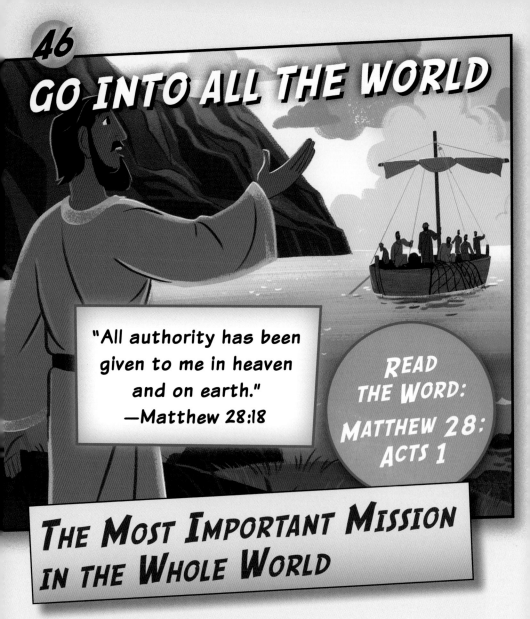

GO INTO ALL THE WORLD

"All authority has been given to me in heaven and on earth."
—Matthew 28:18

READ THE WORD:
MATTHEW 28;
ACTS 1

THE MOST IMPORTANT MISSION IN THE WHOLE WORLD

How would you feel if you were being entrusted with the most important mission in the whole world? You'd probably feel a lot like Jesus's first disciples. For forty days after His resurrection, Jesus had been meeting with them in public and in private. He was teaching and encouraging them for the path ahead of them. This day, though, was different. He called them to a mountain in Galilee. After they worshiped Jesus, they asked when He would begin His kingdom.

But Jesus changed the conversation. The kingdom didn't work that way. It would start small and grow into something incredible that would never fade away. Then Jesus gave them their mission: "Go . . . and make disciples of all nations, baptizing them in the name of the Father and of the Son and of the Holy Spirit, teaching them to observe everything I have commanded you. And . . . I am with you always, to the end of the age" (Matthew 28:19–20).

THE POWER AND PRESENCE OF JESUS

This mission was the most important mission in the whole world. Go and make disciples. Tell others about Jesus. Baptize them. Teach them to obey Him, and train them to continue the mission. This message was so important that Jesus wasn't going to leave them alone to accomplish it. He was going to be with them by sending His Spirit—the Holy Spirit. When the Holy Spirit arrived, He would give Jesus's followers the power to go and make disciples of all nations.

JOINING GOD'S MISSION

Jesus is still giving the call to go and make disciples of all nations. No matter your age, if you believe in Jesus, you have a part to play in God's mission, and He is with you every step of the way.

How does it feel to know that Jesus is always with you? Why?

Who do you want to tell about Jesus? Make a plan to do that this week.

MEMORIZE
2 CORINTHIANS 5:20

"Therefore, we are ambassadors for Christ, since God is making his appeal through us. We plead on Christ's behalf: 'Be reconciled to God.'"

47

THE PROMISED HELPER

READ THE WORD: ACTS 1-2

FILLED BY THE SPIRIT

"Repent and be baptized, each of you, in the name of Jesus Christ for the forgiveness of your sins, and you will receive the gift of the Holy Spirit."—Acts 2:38

It was Pentecost, a festival when the Jews offered the firstfruits of the harvest. The disciples waited and prayed, just as Jesus had commanded before He returned to heaven. They were waiting for the Helper to come: the Holy Spirit who would empower them in the mission to go and make disciples. Suddenly they heard a sound like a violent rushing wind that filled the whole house! When they looked at one another, they saw what looked like flames resting on their heads. The Holy Spirit had come. The disciples left the room where they had gathered and went outside, praising God.

When the Jews in the city—from every nation—heard the disciples, they were confused. Somehow, the people could each hear their own languages and understand what the disciples were saying. But how? Peter said it was God's doing! Then he told them about Jesus—His life, death, and resurrection. The people were amazed and asked what they should do. Peter commanded them to repent, to turn away from their sins and to be baptized in the name of Jesus. And three thousand people became followers of Jesus that day.

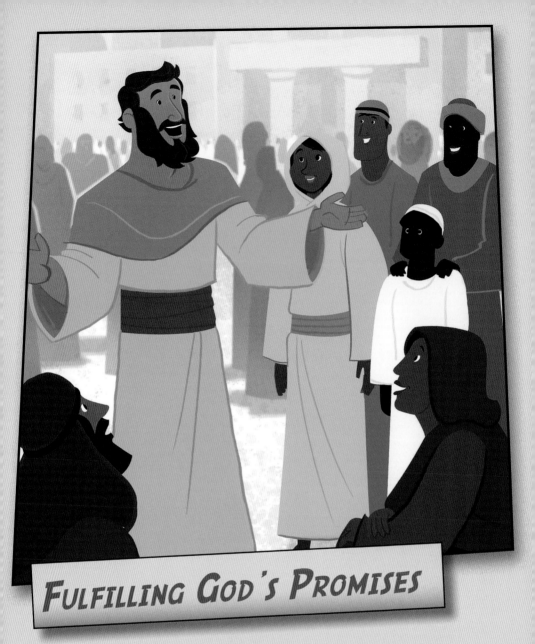

FULFILLING GOD'S PROMISES

When Peter preached to the people, he told them that
Scripture was being fulfilled as God poured out His Spirit on
His servants (Acts 2:18). But this wasn't the only promise
God fulfilled: Jesus was the Messiah, the Rescuer God's
people had been waiting for. Even though they had
sentenced Him to death (Acts 2:36), His death was God's plan
all along to save everyone who put their trust in Jesus.

GOING FORWARD IN THE SPIRIT'S POWER

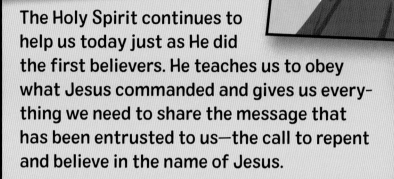

The Holy Spirit continues to help us today just as He did the first believers. He teaches us to obey what Jesus commanded and gives us everything we need to share the message that has been entrusted to us—the call to repent and believe in the name of Jesus.

Is it easy to believe that God always fulfills His promises? Why or why not?

How have you seen the Holy Spirit working in your life?

MEMORIZE ACTS 2:21

"Then everyone who calls on the name of the Lord will be saved."

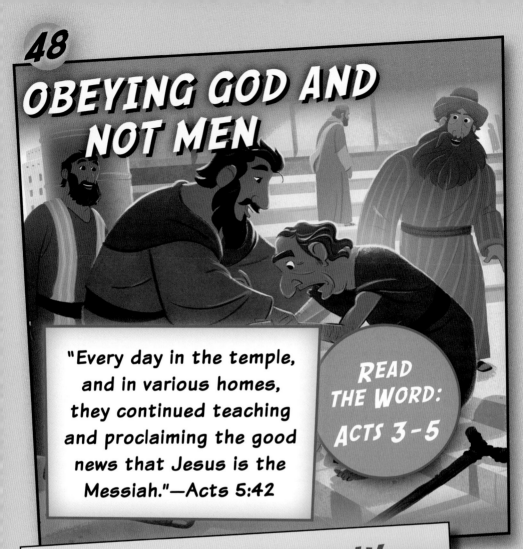

48

OBEYING GOD AND NOT MEN

"Every day in the temple, and in various homes, they continued teaching and proclaiming the good news that Jesus is the Messiah."—Acts 5:42

READ THE WORD: ACTS 3–5

THE POWER OF GOD AT WORK

Every day, more people began to follow Jesus as the apostles taught about what He had done and the people saw the His disciples' love for one another. One day, as Peter and John were going to pray at the temple, they met a man who could not walk. The man asked them for money, but Peter had none. Instead he said, "In the name of Jesus, get up and walk!" Immediately, the man did just that! Everyone who saw what had happened was amazed.

But when the religious leaders learned what happened
and heard Peter and John preaching, they had the two
men arrested. The leaders did not believe that Jesus was
the Messiah or that He had been raised from the dead.
They ordered Peter and John to stop speaking about
Jesus, but the apostles refused. They had to speak; it was
better to obey God than human authorities.

FIGHTING AGAINST GOD

The apostles continued to preach the gospel in Jerusalem and performed many signs and wonders—miracles. They healed the sick. They cast demons out of people. They showed God's power as they proclaimed the good news of Jesus's life, death, and resurrection. More people joined them each day. The religious leaders tried to figure out how to stop the spread of the gospel, but they couldn't. No matter how much they tried, the apostles kept teaching, and more people kept believing. Finally, the leaders realized that if this was a message made up by human beings, it would eventually fail. If it was from God—if it was true—then there was nothing they could do. To try to stop it would be fighting against God.

SPEAKING WHEN IT'S DIFFICULT

Powerful people didn't want the apostles preaching the gospel. Today, we have the same challenge. Talking about Jesus isn't popular, but God wants us to do it because the gospel is the most important message in the whole world.

Imagine you were with Peter and John when they were told to stop talking about Jesus. How do you think you would have felt? Why?

Do you find it easy to share the gospel? Pray that the Holy Spirit would help you tell others about Jesus.

MEMORIZE ROMANS 10:17

"So faith comes from what is heard, and what is heard comes through the message about Christ."

49

THE FIRST MARTYR

> "He knelt down and cried out with a loud voice, 'Lord, do not hold this sin against them!'"
> —Acts 7:60

THE STONING OF STEPHEN

Stephen was a servant in the church who distributed food to widows. He was filled with grace and the Holy Spirit and performed many signs and wonders in the sight of the Jews. But some opposed him as he shared the gospel, and the religious leaders accused him of blasphemy— of telling lies about God. Stephen told them they had always resisted God and that Jesus came to rescue them,

READ THE WORD: ACTS 6-8

but the leaders became furious. They picked up stones and threw them at Stephen. They yelled as loud as they could to drown out his voice. More and more stones hit Stephen, until his voice was silent. Stephen was dead. The religious leaders began to persecute the church, and the disciples fled from Jerusalem.

THE GOSPEL COULDN'T BE STOPPED

Stephen's death could have been the end for the church, but it was only the beginning. The disciples were in danger because of the religious leaders' persecution, and they were scattered from Jerusalem. But nothing could stop the spread of the gospel. Everywhere the disciples went, they shared the gospel with the people they met. People believed in Judea, Samaria, Antioch, Alexandria, Samaria, and beyond. Nothing could stop the gospel because it was the work of God: His plan to rescue and redeem sinners through faith in Jesus Christ.

CONTINUING THE MISSION

Just as God called the first disciples to share the gospel with everyone, He wants to use us to continue sharing the gospel until the day Jesus returns.

How does this story encourage us to keep telling the truth about Jesus even when it's difficult?

Has anyone ever said or done something hurtful to you because of your faith in Jesus? Pray that God would help you show kindness to that person.

MEMORIZE
2 TIMOTHY 1:7

"For God has not given us a spirit of fear, but one of power, love, and sound judgment."

50

FROM PERSECUTOR TO PROCLAIMER

READ THE WORD: ACTS 9-13

"*Go, for this man is my chosen instrument to take my name to Gentiles, kings, and Israelites.*"—Acts 9:15

"WHY DO YOU PERSECUTE ME?"

No one would have expected Saul to start following Jesus. He was the church's greatest persecutor. He had watched as Stephen was killed and had approved of it. He launched a campaign to rid Judea of the Christians. After all, he believed they were blasphemers, worshiping Jesus of Nazareth and calling Him "God." In Saul's eyes, they deserved to die. But then a bright light stopped Paul in his tracks as he raced toward Damascus.

He fell to the ground and heard a voice speaking to him: "Saul, Saul, why are you persecuting me?" (Acts 9:4). It was Jesus. He told Saul to get up and continue on to Damascus and wait there. The light disappeared, but Saul could no longer see. His companions had to lead him to Damascus, where he waited for three days until a man named Ananias, a disciple of Jesus, arrived. Ananias prayed for Saul, and immediately something that looked like scales fell from Saul's eyes. Saul could see—not only Ananias's face, but he could see Jesus for who He really is: the Lord, God Himself!

SIGHT FOR THE BLIND

When Saul's eyes were opened to the truth of the gospel, he immediately joined the other followers of Jesus in sharing the gospel. He had been blind to the truth for so long; now his only desire was for everyone to see the truth about Jesus. He would spend the rest of his life sharing this good news, and he would suffer for the sake of the gospel. Even in suffering, he considered it all worth it. He was once blind, but now he saw the truth: Jesus is God, and our only hope for salvation comes from faith in Him.

DON'T STOP SHARING THE GOOD NEWS!

Saul's desire to share the gospel wasn't unique to him. This desire is the same one the Holy Spirit gives to everyone who believes—a desire for more people to see Jesus for who He really is and put their faith in Him!

Talk to your family about what they thought about Jesus before they believed the gospel. Pray and thank God that He still gives sight to people who are blind to the truth about Jesus.

What are the scariest things to you about sharing the gospel? Why?

MEMORIZE
PHILIPPIANS 3:8

"More than that, I also consider everything to be a loss in view of the surpassing value of knowing Christ Jesus my Lord."

51

"PREACHING WHERE CHRIST HAS NOT BEEN NAMED"

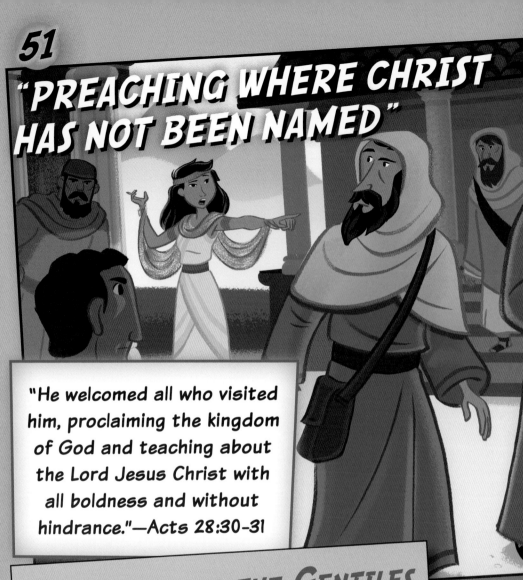

"He welcomed all who visited him, proclaiming the kingdom of God and teaching about the Lord Jesus Christ with all boldness and without hindrance."—Acts 28:30-31

MISSIONARY TO THE GENTILES

A few years after he joined the Christians, Saul (also called Paul) was sent to Cyprus to preach the gospel to the Jews. As he taught from the Scriptures, many were amazed and some believed, but the religious leaders insulted Paul and his companions. Driven out of the synagogues, Paul preached the gospel to the Gentiles, the non-Jewish people of the region—and something incredible happened: they believed!

READ
THE WORD:
ACTS
14-28

Everywhere he went, Paul experienced the same thing: the Jews rejected him, but the Gentiles embraced the gospel with joy. But Paul's journeys were not free from difficulty. He was met with resistance and threats in every city, from both Jews and Gentiles. He faced riots, was stoned and imprisoned, suffered multiple shipwrecks, and was even bitten by a snake! But through it all, Paul preached Christ and encouraged many believers in every city he visited, fulfilling his desire to preach Christ where He had not been named.

THE GOSPEL IS FOR ALL

Although Paul experienced much difficulty and persecution, his ministry was filled with great joy as well. The
gospel was going out into the nations, just as Jesus had
commanded. In every church Paul planted and with every
letter he wrote, he encouraged believers to continue in that
mission. The goal was to see others live from the same
hope he had, the hope that God's promises would be and
are being fulfilled in Jesus, the Son of God—the Rescuer
who would save all who believe from their sins.

GO AND TELL

Through his letters and his example, Paul encourages us to continue on in the mission that drove him: to preach Christ where He had not yet been named. God wants us to share the hope we have in Christ with everyone, until there are no more people who need to hear this good news!

We talk about what we love most. What do you love to do most? What do you love about it?

Many people all over the world are working to spread the gospel. Pray that God would work through them so people from every nation would know Jesus.

MEMORIZE ROMANS 10:15

"And how can they preach unless they are sent? As it is written: How beautiful are the feet of those who bring good news."

52

THE END OF THE BEGINNING

> "Look, I am coming soon! Blessed is the one who keeps the words of the prophecy of this book."
> —Revelation 22:7

READ THE WORD: REVELATION 1-22

A VISION OF THE FUTURE

When John, the last of the apostles, was an old man, he had a vision: he saw a Man dressed in brilliant white clothing, with eyes like lightning, hair as white as snow, and a gold sash around His chest. It was Jesus, in all His glory. He told John that He was going to show him what was to come— the end of the beginning of the story God has been telling throughout history. John saw visions of terrible persecution, beasts, and a great dragon who was the serpent from the garden that tempted the first people. John also saw a great warrior riding a white horse into battle against the dragon: Jesus. The dragon was defeated and thrown into a lake of fire. John saw people from every nation and ethnicity, every color and language, from all times and places. All of them were praising Jesus. Then a heavenly city came down from heaven to the earth, and at the center was the tree of life, which bore fruit every month. All who lived in the city were welcome to eat the fruit of this tree and enjoy life in the presence of God forever and ever, as God had intended from the beginning.

JESUS WINS

When Jesus gave John this vision, He told the elderly apostle to write it all down to encourage all the churches. Jesus wanted them to know that even when they faced terrible difficulties, they should not lose hope because they knew the end of the story—Jesus wins! And Jesus, the King of kings and Lord of lords, will go to each person—every single one who has been saved through faith in Him (Ephesians 2:8). He will wipe the tears from every eye and replace their sadness with joy.

HE IS COMING SOON

Before the vision ended, Jesus promised John that He is coming soon. While Jesus's "soon" doesn't look like ours, we know that He is coming. So while we wait, we can say along with John, "Amen! Come, Lord Jesus!" (Revelation 22:20).

Jesus has already defeated sin forever. How does knowing this give you hope as you fight sin right now?

Do you have a friend who is going through difficult times? How can you encourage your friend with Jesus's promise to make everything new?

MEMORIZE
REVELATION 21:5

"Then the one seated on the throne said, 'Look, I am making everything new.' He also said, 'Write, because these words are faithful and true.'"

REMEMBER

"John saw Jesus coming toward him and said, 'Here is the Lamb of God, who takes away the sin of the world!'"
—John 1:29

READ

Read John 1:1–18. Where does the story of Jesus—the story of the gospel—begin? It's sometimes tempting to think that Jesus's story doesn't really start until Matthew 1:1, the beginning of the New Testament. And that's true in one respect; after all, the account of His birth, life on earth, death, and resurrection are all contained in the four Gospels. They show us people's amazement at His teaching, their awestruck wonder at His miracles, and the religious leaders' anger at His challenges to their teaching.

Although it's true that the four Gospels are the beginning of Jesus's story, it's also not—and it's the Gospels that remind us of this, because in the beginning was God, and with Him was "the Word" (John 1:1), who was God and was the One through whom all things were created (v. 3). The Word who "became flesh and dwelt among us," so that humanity could see His glory, "the glory as the one and only Son from the Father, full of grace and truth" (v. 14).

Jesus, the Word of God, the Son of God, the One whose story is told throughout every page of the Bible, from Genesis to Revelation. And as we go into the world, we are called to tell everyone we meet about Him, the One they need to rescue and redeem them.

THINK

1. What is one of the hardest parts of the Bible for you to understand? Do you look at that part differently when you remember that it reveals something to you about Jesus?

2. Why does it matter that the Bible tells one big story? How does that fact change the way you read and understand it?

3. Think about John the Baptist's words in John 1:29. What do you think was going through his mind when he realized Jesus was the "Lamb of God"?

4. Jesus came to reveal "grace and truth" to us (John 1:17). How does the grace He shows us in the gospel help us to be gracious to others?

5. God wants us to share the gospel with others. Who do you know who doesn't know Jesus? Make a plan to share the good news with him or her.

THE BIBLE ISN'T JUST EXCITING – IT'S EPIC

Are you ready for the story that changed the world? Packed with illustrations, this compelling book lets middle-grade readers rediscover forty Bible narratives, from the creation to the cross and the resurrection to the revelation. Each chapter includes a life-application question to get readers thinking and to show them how all the pieces of the Bible fit together to create one incredible story about the greatest Hero of all.

GET READY FOR THE GREATEST EPIC EVER WRITTEN, AND LET IT POINT YOU TO JESUS.